The Complete Poetry and Prose of Chairil Anwar

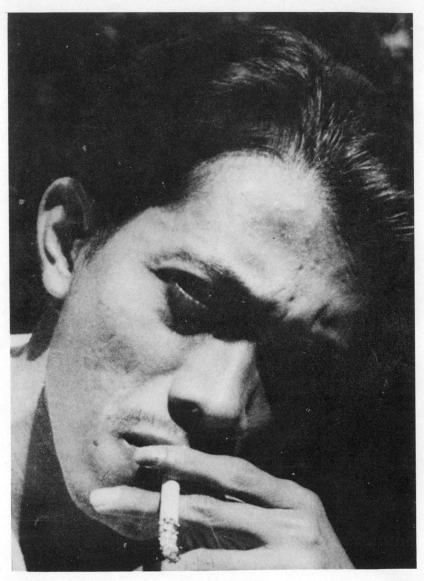

CHAIRIL ANWAR

The Complete Poetry and Prose
of Chairil Anwar

Edited and translated by Burton Raffel

STATE UNIVERSITY OF NEW YORK PRESS

ALBANY

Published by State University of New York Press
Thurlow Terrace, Albany, New York 12201

Standard Book Number 87395-060-7
Library of Congress Catalog Card Number 76-91201
Manufactured in the United States of America

For four different singers:
John Lennon, Paul McCartney,
George Harrison, Richard Starkey

Contents

Acknowledgments xi

Introduction xiii

POETRY

2 . . . . Nisan / Gravestone 3

4 . . . . Penghidupan / Life 5

6 . . . . Dipo Negoro / Dipo Negoro 7

10 . . . . Sia-Sia / In Vain 11

12 . . . . Adjakan / Invitation 13

14 . . . . Sendiri / Alone 15

16 . . . . Pelarian / A Fugitive 17

18 . . . . Suara Malam / The Voice of the Night 19

20 . . . . Aku / Me 21

22 . . . . Hukum / The Law 23

24 . . . . Taman / Our Garden 25

26 . . . . Lagu Biasa / An Ordinary Song 27

28 . . . . Kupu Malam Dan Biniku / A Whore and My Wife 29

30 . . . . Penerimaan / Willingness 31

32 . . . . Kesabaran / Patience 33

34 . . . . Perhitungan / A Reckoning-Up 35

36 . . . . Kenangan / Memories 37

38 . . . . Rumahku / My House 39

40 . . . . Hampa / Empty 41

42 . . . . Kawanku Dan Aku / My Friend and I 43

44 . . . . Bertjerai / Parting 45

46 . . . . Aku / Me (Poem #2) 47

48 . . . . Tjerita / A Story 49

50 . . . . Dimesdjid / At the Mosque 51

52 . . . . Kepada Peminta-Minta / To a Beggar 53

54 . . . . Selamat Tinggal / Goodbye 55
56 . . . . (untitled) / Your Mouth 57
58 . . . . Dendam / Revenge 59
60 . . . . Merdeka / Free 61
62 . . . . (untitled) / We Wobble Along 63
64 . . . . ? / ? 65
66 . . . . 1943 / 1943 67
68 . . . . Isa / Jesus Christ 69
70 . . . . Doa / Prayer 71
72 . . . . Sadjak Putih / A Pure Rhyme 73
74 . . . . Dalam Kereta / In the Train 75
76 . . . . Siap-Sedia / We're Ready 77
80 . . . . Kepada Penjair Bohang / For the Poet Bohang 81
82 . . . . Lagu Siul / Whistling Song 83
84 . . . . Malam / Evening 85
86 . . . . Orang Berdua / Together 87
88 . . . . Sebuah Kamar / A Room 89
90 . . . . Kepada Pelukis Affandi / To the Painter Affandi 91
92 . . . . Tjatetan Th. 1946 / Notes for 1946 93
94 . . . . Buat Album D.S. / D.S.: For her Album 95
96 . . . . Nocturno (Fragment) / Nocturno: A Fragment 97
98 . . . . Tjerita Buat Dien Tamaela / A Tale for Dien Tamaela 99
102 . . . . Kabar Dari Laut / News from the Sea 103
104 . . . . Sendja Di Pelabuhan Ketjil / Twilight at a Little Harbor 105
106 . . . . Tjintaku Djauh Dipulau / My Love's on a Faraway Island 107
108 . . . . "Betina"—nja Affandi / Affandi's Slut 109
110 . . . . Situasi / Situation 111
112 . . . . Dari Dia / From Her 113
114 . . . . Kepada Kawan / To a Friend 115
116 . . . . Pemberian Tahu / A Proclamation 117
118 . . . . Sadjak Buat Basuki Resobowo / Poem for Basuki Resobowo 119
120 . . . . Sorga / Heaven 121
122 . . . . Malam Di Pegunungan / Evening in the Mountains 123
124 . . . . Tuti Artic / Tuti's Ice Cream 125
126 . . . . Krawang-Bekasi / Krawang-Bekasi 127
130 . . . . Persetudjuan Dengan Bung Karno / Agreement with Friend Soekarno 131

132 . . . . (untitled) / Like This 133
134 . . . . Ina Mia / Ina Mia 135
136 . . . . Perdjurit Djaga Malam / A Sentry at Night 137
138 . . . . Puntjak / On Top of the Mountain 139
140 . . . . Buat Gadis Rasid / For Miss Gadis Rasid 141
142 . . . . (untitled) / While the Moon Gleams 143
144 . . . . Aku Berkisar Antara Mereka / I Run Around with Them 145
146 . . . . Buat Njonja N. / For Mrs. N. 147
148 . . . . Mirat Muda, Chariril Muda / Mirat's Young, Chairil's Young 149
150 . . . . Jang Terampas Dan Jang Luput / Some are Plundered, Some Escape 151
152 . . . . Derai-Derai Tjemara / Fir Trees in Rows 153
154 . . . . (untitled) / Let This Evening Go By 155
156 . . . . (untitled) / I'm Back Again 157
158 . . . . (untitled) / Let's Leave Here 159

PROSE

Three Against Fate 163
An Untitled Speech: 1943 163
Looking it in the Eye 170
Hoppla! 174
Writing Poems, Looking at Pictures 176
Radio Talk, 1946 178
Three Approaches, One Idea 181
Four Aphorisms 184
Excerpts from Letters to H. B. Jassin 185

APPENDIXES AND BIBLIOGRAPHY

A: Notes on the Indonesian Originals 189
B: Notes on the English Versions 199
Bibliography 205

Acknowledgments

To Pembangunan, Pustaka Rakjat, and Balai Pustaka, all of Djakarta, publishers of Chairil Anwar's three volumes of verse; to Gunung Agung, Djakarta, publishers of H. B. Jassin's bibliographical study, which prints poems not elsewhere available; to the magazine *Ipphos Report,* for copies of three poems not anywhere else in print, and to Professor A. Teeuw, of Leiden, who sent me another copy of one of these; to H. B. Jassin of Djakarta, for the photograph of Anwar appearing on the dust jacket; to Frank D. Underwood, Cultural Affairs Officer at the U.S. Embassy in Djakarta, for helping to contact Jassin; to Arsath Ro'is for the Frontispiece photo; to Professor John M. Echols, of Cornell University, who taught me Indonesian in the first place, and who has continued to answer calls for help of all sorts; to Professor Anthony H. Johns, of the Australian National University, for helpful comments and criticisms; to Nurdin Salam, with whom I worked on early versions of many of these poems; and to Mia Raffel, who read every translation with wonderfully balanced sensitivity. All of the prose pieces appeared, sometimes in slightly different form, in the "Appendix of Indonesian Literary Opinion" in Raffel, *The Development of Modern Indonesian Poetry,* pp. 219–236.

Introduction

Chairil Anwar was born in Medan, Sumatra, on 26 July 1922. His family does not seem to have been a wealthy or a prominent one, but the fact that Anwar completed elementary school (six years) and the first two years of the Dutch lower middle school, M.U.L.O. (*Meer Uitgebreid Lager Onderwijs*), indicates at least moderate prosperity. Not many Indonesians, in what was then the Dutch East Indies, were able to have any higher education, since such schooling was extraordinarily expensive; even had the money been available, even fewer Indonesians had the requisite degree of Dutch culture. For the teaching was entirely in Dutch, the books were entirely in Dutch, and the teachers were either Dutch or rigorously trained to seem Dutch. "Quite apart from the nature of the instruction given—and as a rule it came into sharp conflict with the traditional native conceptions—the mere fact of its existence made a breach in the agrarian structure. . . . The social prestige and the comparative material prosperity attached to an 'intellectual' position were so attractive that many simple people endured the greatest sacrifices in order to afford their children the advantages of a reasonably good education." (Wertheim, *Indonesian Society in Transition,* 2nd ed, The Hague, 1959, pp. 145–146.)

Anwar's family seems to have lost whatever money it had before he could finish his education. In 1940, two years before the Japanese Occupation began, he left Sumatra and came to Djakarta (then Batavia). He does not seem to have had a job, or any intention of beginning what is conventionally thought of as a career. The communal structure of Indonesian society, the omnipresence of relatives and relatives of relatives, as well as the comparatively low standard of living—much lower in 1940 than after World War II, and independence—made it possible to sustain oneself for months, for years, without fixed occupation or resources. When, for example, the young writer Ajip Rosidi (1938–   ) first came to Djakarta in 1951, he lived with an uncle:

Ours was a row house, and the portion rented by my uncle was the very finest available. The rest was inhabited by all sorts of people: messengers, ice-peddlers, pedicab drivers, cigarette vendors, train conductors, and some others who worked at trades I never learned about. Measuring roughly thirty-three by twenty-three feet, the house had a total of fifty-seven inhabitants. If sometimes there were guests from the country, the total went higher. I had to sleep in an iron bed, along with two other men. A room about ten feet by seven had five people living in it. (Rosidi in Raffel, *The Development of Modern Indonesian Poetry,* p. 257.)

In a sense, Anwar *did* nothing the rest of his life (he died 28 April 1949):

Because he lived so restlessly, he could not endure working in an office, chained to a desk every day. When he was asked what he worked at, he answered "I'm a Poet." His residence was not fixed, he moved from one place to another, from one friend's house to another, from one hotel to another. . . . [He was] a thin, pale youngster, careless of his appearance. His eyes were red, and very wild, but they always appeared thoughtful; his movements were slow, as if utterly indifferent. . . . In his ideals, in his movements, and in his actions themselves, he stabbed, cut, and smashed old notions, leading some of his friends to think him ignorant, unaware of custom, a kind of bandit, characterizations he himself thought an honor and necessary in order to influence his slower friends into revolutionary ways. . . . A typical remark: 'When I die I don't want it to be in a bed. I want to die in the middle of the street.' (H. B. Jassin, in Raffel, op. cit., pp. 80–81, 88.)

Different friends have equally vivid and extraordinarily different memories of him. One remembers him riding in an open car, perched high, and shouting verses of Emily Dickinson into the wind. Another remembers that, wanting to know what it was like to make love in public, Anwar hired a prostitute, went to a public park, and made love. Still another remembers the time, under the Japanese Occupation, when the police, trying to track down some active resistance people, briefly arrested and tortured Anwar, who was suspected of knowing useful names and addresses. He in fact did know them, though he was not himself actively involved in resistance any more than he was in anything but his writing. After a very brief time spent hanging with his arms bent behind him, Anwar told the Japanese everything he knew. "I couldn't help it," he is quoted as saying afterward—not so much in apology as in complete explanation—"it hurt too much."

To say that Anwar was not the stuff of which resistance fighters is made is not to denigrate him. It serves no purpose to set him up as a guerrilla fighter, a gun-toting militant, a Fidel Castro, or Mao Tse Tung. Anwar spoke the plain truth: "I'm a Poet." Even editorial work, for which he might have been (but was not) temperamentally suited, could not hold him. "The longest stint 'in the office' was, for him, when he joined the editorial board of [the magazine] *Gema Suasana* (*Echoes from All Over*), but this was only for three months and in that time he was in the office on only a few occasions." I am quoting H. B. Jassin, the critic, close friend of, and leading Indonesian authority on Anwar. "He clearly could not set restrictions on others, nor on himself; his desires exceeded the bounds of what is possible in this life. Neither could he tie himself down to family life, although his marriage did produce a daughter. The world was too vast and a house too tiny for tasting all of life's pleasures." (H. Jassin, in Raffel, *op.cit.*, p. 90.)

The details of Anwar's life, from his arrival in Djakarta in 1940 until his death nine years later, are not hard to imagine. When he died he had long suffered from syphilis and he had tuberculosis, typhus, and cirrhosis of the liver as well. The young poet W. S.

Rendra (1935–   ), although nominally discussing the nature of "inspiration," gives what seems a very likely, if somewhat colored picture of Anwar's activities:

Among writers, and especially among younger writers, there is something called "hunting for inspiration." What in fact is meant by this is that they wander around at night, sit for a long time in coffeehouses and waste time with empty gossip, flit around in red-light districts, with their clothing dirty from sitting in sidewalk cafés far into the small hours, hang about and chat, leaning on bridge rails, and employ a variety of other devices, all equally odd. This sort of thing developed rapidly as an inheritance from the Generation of '45, and especially from Chairil Anwar. (Rendra, in Raffel, *op.cit.,* p. 253.)

These "odd" ways were plainly accentuated by the enormous social dislocation caused by the coming of the Japanese—and their almost ludicrously easy dislodging of the Dutch. Decades of belief in the virtual omnipotence of Dutch might, of growing respect for and determination to participate in Western patterns of social and economic existence, were shaken. It was hard, in spite of Japanese fanaticism and harshness, not to admire a fellow Oriental people for what they had determined to do and then *done.*"A brave warrior," said Anwar enthusiastically of Japanese Colonel Jamasaki, "[a] noble spirit. The personification of the ideal!" (See "An Untitled Speech: 1943," ["*Pidato,* 1943"] p. 163.) All the normal patterns of colonial Indonesian society were disrupted; no one could know for sure where anything was going. In a joint statement issued on 19 November 1946, upon the founding of *Gelanggang* (*The Arena*), Anwar joined with others to assert that "This generation was born out of our struggles, in life and in thought, while engaged in creating the new, the fully alive Indonesian man. . . . We wish to free ourselves from the old system that has weakened our nation, nor are we afraid to challenge the old views, the old ways, in order to ignite new and powerful fires." (*Ibid.,* pp. 249–250.)

This same challenge was aimed at the "old" literary generation, the *Pudjangga Baru* (*New Writer*) school of the 1930s. Much of *Pudjangga Baru* writing was romantic and idealistic, "utterly bland," as Anwar rather harshly wrote in 1945. (See "Hoppla," p. 174.) More typically, he had written two years earlier, that these people achieve only "warm chicken shit!! . . . Till now our art has been thin, superficial. No more of the old farts. No more gentle breezes of *that* kind!" ("An Untitled Speech: 1943," p. 163.) He spoke all the more fervently, perhaps, because his own early poetry, written before his arrival in Djakarta, was composed on *Pudjangga Baru* models. None of this imitative verse survives; it is said that Anwar destroyed it, which seems very likely.

Anwar's more mature concern (his first great poetry was written at age twenty!) was "to reach an absolute accounting with everything around me." (Letter of 8 March 1944, p. 185.) "From the time I was fifteen years old I've headed for only one goal: art." (Letter, p. 185.) I think it is fair to say that his relentless and obsessively dedicated pursuit of this "one goal" sets Chairil Anwar apart from every Indonesian writer who preceded him. And the fact of the matter is that the Generation of '45 *is* Chairil Anwar's Generation—indeed, the novelist Achdiat K. Mihardja has written an article entitled, *tout court*, "Angkatan '45: Angkatan Chairil, Angkatan Merdeka" ("The Generation of '45: Chairil's Generation, The Generation of Freedom"; for a translation, see Raffel, *op.cit.*, pp. 236–243.) Anwar transformed both the Indonesian literary scene and the Indonesian language. Nor was this explosive opening of doors confined to poetry. Modern Indonesian literature was born with the work of Chairil Anwar.

One can attempt to document that kind of achievement, outline its boundaries. Its chemistry is beyond all analysis.

———————

I have spoken of Anwar's need for absolute honesty, of his drive toward revolutionary methods of feeling and of expression. These were in a sense what enabled him to be the spiritual leader of his generation. What actually made him that leader was his ability to exploit the Indonesian language, to create effects so stunning that even some of his fellow poets have admitted that they did not know what the language could do until they had seen Anwar's work.

> Bung Karno! Kau dan aku satu zat satu urat
> Dizatmu dizatku kapal-kapal kita berlajar
> Diuratmu diuratku kapal-kapal kita berlajar
> Diuratmu diuratku kapal-kapal kita bertolak & berlabuh.

This is the final quatrain, and the climax, of a poem about ex-President Soekarno. The play of "zat" and "urat," joined with a host of related sound repetitions—such as that of the first vowel in "kapal-kapal," which, like everything else in this quatrain, Anwar obviously delights in saying over and over—create a bold, unprecedented aural pattern of finger-snapping boisterousness. And the words match their sounds:

Friend Soekarno! You and me, we're cut from the same plug, we've got the same guts
Our ships sail in your plug and in my plug
Our ships sail in your guts and in my guts
Our ships pull up and drop anchor in your guts and in my guts too.

An undated photostat of what seems to be an early fair copy of the poem shows that this quatrain originally lacked its second line. The sound repetitions gained by adding it are not, strictly speaking, necessary; the effect is pretty much the same without the second line—but with that line the effect is indelibly, memorably underlined. "Improvised art," Anwar wrote in 1943, "is nothing compared to art produced by creative power, by thought, by concentration." And then he added—truthful as usual—"To me this is life and death itself!" ("Looking It In the Eye" [Berhadapan Mata"] p. 170.)

xviii

There were those among the older generations who claimed, falsely, that Chairil Anwar wrote easily, even flippantly. In fact he wrote slowly, painfully. There are seventy-five poems in this book, four of them free adaptations of poems in other languages and one an unrevised bit from a notebook; this is the whole of Anwar's original poetry. Since his active writing career covered roughly seven years, this makes approximately ten poems per year—hardly prolific for a man who had only this "one goal," and who sacrificed to it virtually everything that one thinks of as desirable in life, not excluding life itself. The blunt directness he always sought after meant, for him as for many avant-garde writers in Western countries, a virtual identity between art and artist. The poet must live his poetry, be his poetry. "Everything," said Anwar in a 1946 radio talk, "everything that goes into the making of this fundamental, essential way *must* be experienced, endured (in his spirit, his aspirations, his emotions, his thoughts, and his own knowledge of life) by the poet himself—must become a part of him, of his gladness and sadness, *his* possessions, belonging to his spirit." (see p. 178.)

Anwar's ability to exploit Indonesian included an incredibly acute ear, a power for turning deceptively simple half-sentences into rhythmic structures of immense and lasting power:

> Sudah itu kita sama termangu
> Saling bertanja: Apakah ini?
> Tjinta? Keduanja tak mengerti.
>
> Sehari itu kita bersama. Tak hampir-menghampiri.

> We were stunned
> And asked each other: what's this?
> Love? Neither of us understood.

That day we were together.
We did not touch.

His terse lyricism can be even more condensed:

Ia mengerling. Ia ketawa
Dan rumput kering terus menjala
Ia berkata. Suaranja njaring tinggi
Darahku terhenti berlari.

She winks. She laughs
And the dry grass blazes up.
She speaks. Her voice is loud
My blood stops running.

In a posthumously published article, Anwar makes his rhythmic concerns very explicit:

The tools and devices with which the poet can express himself are the materials of language, which he uses *intuitively*. By "manipulating" the lofty and the low he can achieve a pattern, an organization, and then he can create variations within the pattern—using rhythm as a unifying element. The melody of words can help establish a poem's force as language becomes now heavy and slow, now light and quick. ("Writing Poems, Looking at Pictures" [Membuat Sadjak, Melihat Lukisan], p. 176.)

Although in this article Anwar was consciously discussing the differences between poetry and painting, it is not accidental that the art of music furnishes his critical metaphor. Poetry's links with music lie at the core of its power: without a fine and discriminating ear, a poet is ultimately buried under his own weight. (I think, myself, that Matthew Arnold is the outstanding example of this, in English poetry.)

Not that Anwar neglected the resources of syntax, or the sometimes fiercely compact genius of Indonesian. In the following line, for example, the material before the comma, in English, translates the material before the comma, in Indonesian, in approximately equal space—but then the capabilities of the two languages diverge sharply:

Rambutku ikal menjinar, kau senapsu dulu kuhela

My wavy hair will shine, and you'll be as passionate as you were the last time I drew you to me

I felt impelled, at this point, to whittle down the last half of the line. I tried, but I could not, in justice to the original: everything in the translation is there, in the Indonesian. Nothing has been padded.

Although no comprehensive study has been made of the literary influences on Chairil Anwar, especially influences from foreign literatures, it has often been noted how he drew on foreign vocabularies—Dutch, English, and other languages of the Indonesian archipelago—to enrich an image or change the tone of a line. He also drew on specific foreign poems and poets, sometimes openly, sometimes silently. This is so common a practice, in this century especially, that it would not need mentioning were it not for the fact that, toward the end of his life, pressed for money (mostly for medical bills) and consistently offered more for original poetry than for translations, Anwar signed his own name to a number of translated poems. Even this would not need mentioning were it not for the literary (and political) tempest created after his death, when these plagiarisms were discovered. A full-scale attempt at literary assassination occurred: Anwar stood for things which made the forces of "socialist realism" anxious to turn him into a non-person, an un-poet. (For a fuller discussion, see Raffel, *op.cit.,* pp. 91–96, 140–142, 150–152.) The attempt did not succeed, though it was powerfully mounted. But it is still having literary echoes: most people writing about Anwar, in virtually all languages, seem to feel impelled to discuss the plagiarism issue at some length, and frequently with a degree of defensiveness which, I am convinced, is misplaced.

For Anwar's poetry is as alive, today, as twenty years ago when Anwar himself died. More alive, it seems to me, since literary studies have, since then, clearly established the canon of his work, and have also begun to define its achievements. More alive, too, as his work has begun to find its way into other languages, and to influence poets working in those languages. It is not poetry one forgets, once having known it: an Indonesian doctor, casually met in a Philadelphia garage, surprised me by quoting Anwar in great (and accurate) chunks; an American woman, long resident in Indonesia, came out of anaesthesia, after an operation, and heard herself reciting, over and over, "aku mau hidup seribu tahun lagi" ("I want to live another thousand years")—the final line of Anwar's "Me" ("Aku"). If it is impossible to duplicate his achievement in any other language, it is at least possible to suggest it. He remains Indonesia's greatest literary figure; he deserves a significant and lasting place in Asian and in world literature.

Haifa, Israel
January 1969

The Complete Poetry and Prose of Chairil Anwar

Poetry

NISAN

Untuk nenekanda

Bukan kematian benar menusuk kalbu
Keridlaanmu menerima segala tiba
Tak kutahu setinggi itu atas debu
dan duka maha tuan bertachta.

GRAVESTONE

for my Grandfather

It's not death, no, that stabs at my heart
But your willingness to go.
Nor do I know how high
You are, now, supreme over dust, over sorrow.

October 1942

PENGHIDUPAN

Lautan maha dalam
mukul dentur selama
ngudji tenaga pematang kita

mukul dentur selama
hingga hantjur remuk redam
Kurnia Bahgia
ketjil setumpuk
sia-sia dilindung, sia-sia dipupuk.

LIFE

The bottomless ocean
Is always banging
Testing the strength of our dikes

Always banging
Until it smashes to bits
The Blessing of Happiness
A little heap
Cultivated, watched over
In vain.

December 1942

DIPO NEGORO

Dimana pembangunan ini
tuan hidup kembali

Dan bara kagum mendjadi api

Didepan sekali tuan menanti
Tak gentar. Lawan banjaknja seratus kali.
Pedang dikanan, keris dikiri
Berselempang semangat jang tak bisa mati.

Madju

Ini barisan tak bergenderang-berpalu
Kepertjajaan tanda menjerbu.

Sekali berarti
Sudah itu mati.

Madju

Bagimu Negeri
Menjediakan api.

Punah diatas menghamba
Binasa diatas ditinda
Sungguhpun dalam adjal baru tertjapai
Djika hidup harus merasai.

DIPO NEGORO *

In this time of building, forging
You live again

And astonished embers burn

You're waiting far ahead
Fearless. A hundred hundred enemies.
Your right hand has a sword, your left hand has a dagger
And your soul has what can never die

Forward

These soldiers beat no drums
They show their faith by attacking

To mean something, once
Then death

Forward

For your country
You lit a fire

Better destruction than slavery
Better extermination than oppression
It may come after our death
But life has to be life

Madju.
Serbu.
Serang.
Terdjang.

-century hero in the Indonesian national

SIA-SIA

Penghabisan kali itu kau datang
membawa karangan kembang
Mawar merah dan melati putih:
darah dan sutji.
Kau tebarkan depanku
serta pandang jang memastikan: Untukmu.

Sudah itu kita sama termangu
Saling bertanja: Apakah ini?
Tjinta? Keduanja tak mengerti.

Sehari itu kita bersama. Tak hampir-menghampiri.

Ah! Hatiku jang tak mau memberi
Mampus kau dikojak-kojak sepi.

IN VAIN

The last time you came
You brought flowers,
Red roses, white jasmine,
Blood and holiness,
And spread them in front of me
With a wondering look: for you.

We were stunned
And asked each other: what's this?
Love? Neither of us understood.

That day we were together.
We did not touch.

But oh my heart that will not give itself
Break, you bastard, ripped by your loneliness!

February 1943

ADJAKAN

Ida
Menembus sudah tjaja
Udara tebal kabut
Katja hitam lumut
Petjah-pentjar sekarang
Diruang legah lapang
Mari ria lagi
Tudjuh belas tahun kembali
Bersepeda sama-gandingan
Kita djalani ini djalan
Ria bahgia
Tak atjuh apa-apa
Gembira-girang
Biar hudjan datang
Kita mandi-basahkan diri
Tahu pasti sebentar kering lagi

INVITATION

Ida,
The sun has pushed through
The air that's thick with fog,
The mouldy black mirror
Has cracked and blown away.
In this great open chamber
Let's be happy again
Be seventeen again
Let's ride side by side
Let's take this road

Gay and happy
Not caring about anything
Excited and pleased.
Let it rain
We'll get ourselves soaked
Knowing how soon we'll be dry again.

February 1943

SENDIRI

Hidupnja tambah sepi, tambah hampa
Malam apa lagi
Ia memekik ngeri
Ditjekik kesunjian kamarnja

Ia membentji. Dirinja dari segala
Jang minta perempuan untuk kawannja

Bahaja dari tiap sudut. Mendekat djuga
Dalam ketakutan-menanti ia menjebut satu nama

Terkedjut ia terduduk. Siapa memanggil itu?
Ah! Lemah lesu ia tersedu: Ibu! Ibu!

ALONE

His life becomes lonelier, emptier
Especially at night
He screams with fear
Choked by the silence in his room

He is full of hate. And mostly for himself
For chasing skirts

The danger comes from every corner. It comes closer.
In the terror of waiting he calls out a single name

Startled, he slumps down. Who said that?
Ah! Feebly, wearily, he sobs: Momma! Momma!

February 1943

PELARIAN

I

Tak tertahan lagi
remang miang sengketa disini.

Dalam lari
Dihempaskannja pintu keras tak berhingga.

Hantjur-luluh sepi seketika
Dan paduan dua djiwa.

II

Dari kelam ke malam
Tertawa-meringis malam menerimanja
Ini batu baru tertjampung dalam gelita
"Mau apa? Raju dan pelupa,
Aku ada! Pilih sadja!
Budjuk dibeli?
Atau sungai sunji?
Mari! Mari!
Turut sadja!"

Tak kuasa—terengkam
Ia ditjengkam malam.

A FUGITIVE

I

The stiff, itching hair of this quarrel
Is no longer bearable

Running,
He slams the door violently

Silence (and the oneness of two hearts)
Is suddenly smashed

II

From twilight to night
The evening welcomes him, grinning.
Another stone drops in the dark.
"What does he want? Tears and then it's done?
I'm here! Just make up your mind!
Flattery bought and paid for?
Or a lonely river?
Come! Come!
Be with me!"

He can't—marooned, drifting
Caught by the night.

February 1943

SUARA MALAM

Dunia badai dan topan
Manusia mengingatkan "Kebakaran dihutan."
Djadi kemana
untuk damai dan reda?
Mati.
Barang kali ini diam kaku sadja
dengan ketenangan selama bersatu
mengatasi suka dan duka
kekebalan terhadap debu dan nafsu.
Berbaring tak sedar
Seperti kapal petjah didasar lautan
djemu dipukul ombak besar.
Atau ini.
Peleburan dalam Tiada
dan sekali akan menghadap tjahaja.
. . . .

Ja Allah! Badanku terbakar—segala samar.
Aku sudah melewati batas.
Kembali? Pintu tertutup dengan keras.

THE VOICE OF THE NIGHT

The world of hurricanes and storms
Makes one think of "Forest Fire." *
And where can we hunt for
Peace and calm?
Death.
Perhaps this silence is only stiff,
Calm while in one piece,
Rising above pleasure and sorrow,
Immune to dust and desire.
To lie down unconscious
Like a broken ship at the bottom of the ocean
Beaten by monotonous waves.
Or this:
Dissolving into Nothingness
And just once facing the light.
. . . .
Oh God! My body is on fire—everything is blurred.
I've gone too far.
Come back? The door is slamming with a loud crash.

February 1943

---

* "Forest Fire," a painting by R. Saleh, shows wild animals being trapped
between death in a forest fire and death in an adjoining ravine.

AKU

Kalau sampai waktuku
'Ku mau tak seorang 'kan meraju
Tidak djuga kau

Tak perlu sedu sedan itu

Aku ini binatang djalang
Dari kumpulannja terbuang

Biar peluru menembus kulitku
Aku tetap meradang menerdjang

Luka dan bisa kubawa berlari
Berlari
Hingga hilang pedih peri

Dan aku akan lebih tidak perduli

Aku mau hidup seribu tahun lagi

ME

When my time comes
I want to hear no one's cries
Nor yours either

Away with all who cry!

Here I am, a wild beast
Driven out of the herd

Bullets may pierce my skin
But I'll keep on,

Carrying forward my wounds and my pain,
Attacking,
Attacking
Until suffering disappears

And I won't care anymore

I want to live another thousand years

March 1943

HUKUM

Saban sore ia lalu depan rumahku
Dalam badju tebal abu-abu

Seorang djerih memikul. Banjak menangkis pukul.

Bungkuk djalannja—Lesu
Putjat mukanja—Lesu

Orang menjebut satu nama djaja
Mengingat kerdjanja dan Djasa

Meletjut supaja terus ini padanja

Tapi mereka memaling. Ia begitu kurang tenaga

Pekik diangkasa: Perwira muda
Pagi ini menjinar lain masa

Nanti, kau dinanti-dimengerti!

THE LAW

Every afternoon he goes by my house
In his heavy grey coat

A man weary with burdens. Parrying many blows.

He stoops—Exhausted
His face pale—Drained

They call out a single triumphant name
Talk about *his* Work, *his* Accomplishment

Whipping him to carry on

But then they turn away. He hasn't the strength

Shouts in the air: Young warrior,
This morning there's a different time shining

Later, you'll be welcomed, you'll be understood!

March 1943

TAMAN

Taman punja kita berdua
tak lebar luas, ketjil sadja
satu tak kehilangan lain dalamnja.
Bagi kau dan aku tjukuplah
Taman kembangnja tak berpuluh warna
Padang rumputnja tak berbanding permadani
halus lembut dipidjak kaki.
Bagi kita itu bukan halangan.
Karena
dalam taman punja berdua
Kau kembang, aku kumbang
aku kumbang, kau kembang.
Ketjil, penuh surja taman kita
tempat merenggut dari dunia dan 'nusia

OUR GARDEN

Our garden
Doesn't spread out very far, it's a little affair
In which we won't lose each other.
For you and me it's enough.
The flowers in our garden don't riot in color
The grass isn't like a carpet
Soft and smooth to walk on.
For us it doesn't matter
Because
In our garden
You're the flower, I'm the bee
I'm the bee, you're the flower.
It's small, it's full of sunlight, this garden of ours,
A place where we draw away from the world, and from people.

March 1943

LAGU BIASA

Diteras rumah makan kami kini berhadapan
Baru berkenalan. Tjuma berpandangan
Sungguhpun samudra djiwa sudah selam berselam

Masih sadja berpandangan
Dalam lakon pertama
Orkes meningkah dengan "Carmen" pula.

Ia mengerling. Ia ketawa
Dan rumput kering terus menjala
Ia berkata. Suaranja njaring tinggi
Darahku terhenti berlari.

Ketika orkes memulai "Ave Maria"
Kuseret ia kesana . . . . . .

AN ORDINARY SONG

On the restaurant terrace, now, we're face to face
Just introduced. We simply stare
Although we've already dived into the ocean of each other's souls

In this first act
We're still only looking
The orchestra plays "Carmen" along with us

She winks. She laughs
And the dry grass blazes up.
She speaks. Her voice is loud
My blood stops running.

When the orchestra begins the "Ave Maria"
I drag her over there . . . . . .

March 1943

KUPU MALAM DAN BINIKU

Sambil berselisih lalu
mengebu debu.

Kupertjepat langkah. Tak noleh kebelakang
Ngeri ini luka-terbuka sekali lagi terpandang

Barah ternganga

Melajang ingatan kebiniku
Lautan jang belum terduga
Biar lebih kami tudjuh tahun bersatu

Barangkali tak setahuku
Ia menipu.

A WHORE AND MY WIFE

As we brushed by each other
Dust got into my eyes

I walked faster. I didn't look back
It was horrible to see that open wound again

A gaping pus-hole

My mind drifted back to my wife
Still a bottomless ocean
Though we've been together seven years

Maybe without my knowing it
She's thrown some dust in my eyes too?

March 1943

PENERIMAAN

Kalau kau mau kuterima kau kembali
Dengan sepenuh hati

Aku masih tetap sendiri

Kutahu kau bukan jang dulu lagi
Bak kembang sari sudah terbagi

Djangan tunduk! Tentang aku dengan berani

Kalau kau mau kuterima kau kembali
Untukku sendiri tapi

Sedang dengan tjermin aku enggan berbagi.

WILLINGNESS

If you like I'll take you back
With all my heart

I'm still alone

I know you're not what you were,
Like a flower pulled into parts

Don't crawl! Stare at me bravely

If you like I'll take you back
For myself, but

I won't share even with a mirror.

March 1943

KESABARAN

Aku tak bisa tidur
Orang ngomong, andjing nggonggong
Dunia djauh mengabur
Kelam mendinding batu
Dihantam suara bertalu-talu
Disebelahnja api dan abu

Aku hendak bitjara
Suaraku hilang, tenaga terbang
Sudah! tidak djadi apa-apa!
Ini dunia enggan disapa, ambil perduli

Keras membeku air kali
Dan hidup bukan hidup lagi

Kuulangi jang dulu kembali
Sambil bertutup telinga, berpitjing mata
Menunggu reda jang mesti tiba

PATIENCE

I can't sleep.
People chatter, dogs bark
The world blurs into the distance
Darkness walled in by stone
Voices batter from one side
Fire and dust from the other

I want to speak
My voice disappears, my strength fades away
Enough! It doesn't matter!
The world refuses to acknowledge me, I don't care

River water turns to ice
And life is life no longer

I do again what I did before
Cover my ears, my eyes
Waiting for the calm that has to come.

April 1943

PERHITUNGAN

Banjak gores belum terputus sadja
Satu rumah ketjil putih dengan lampu merah muda tjaja

Langit bersih-tjerah dan purnama raja . . . . . .
Sudah itu tempatku tak tentu dimana.

Sekilap pandangan serupa dua klewang bergeseran

Sudah itu berlepasan dengan sedikit heran
Hambus kau aku tak perduli, ke Bandung, ke Sukabumi . . . . . . !?
Kini aku meringkih dalam malam sunji.

A RECKONING-UP

There are lines—many—I still haven't cut through
One small white house with a pink lamp burning

A clear bright sky and a huge full moon . . . . . .
After that I don't know the way

A flash of vision like two sabers clanging

Then we run off, a little dazed
You've bolted—to Bandung, to Sukabumi: who cares . . . . . . !?
Now I'm flat, deflated here in the lonely night.

April 1943

35

KENANGAN

untuk Karinah Moordjono

Kadang
Diantara djeridji itu itu sadja
Mereksmi memberi warna
Benda usang dilupa
Ah! tertjebar rasanja diri
Membubung tinggi atas kini
Sedjenak
Sadja. halus rapuh ini djalinan kenang
Hantijur hilang belum dipegang
Terhentak
Kembali diitu-itu sadja
Djiwa bertanja: Dari buah
Hidup kan banjakan djatuh ketanah?
Menjelubung njesak penjesalan pernah menjia-njia

MEMORIES

for Karinah Moordjono

Sometimes
On these same old bars
Something withered and forgotten
Bursts in full color.
Ah! The shock
Of it floating up
For just
A moment. This wisp of recollection
Dissolves before it can be caught
Snapping back
To that unchanging sameness.
The soul asks: Of the fruits of life
Don't most drop to the earth?
Regret smothers frustration.

April 1943

RUMAHKU

Rumahku dari unggun-timbun sadjak
Katja djernih dari luar segala nampak

Kulari dari gedong lebar halaman
Aku tersesat tak dapat djalan

Kemah kudirikan ketika sendjakala
Dipagi terbang entah kemana

Rumahku dari unggun-timbun sadjak
Disini aku berbini dan beranak

Rasanja lama lagi, tapi datangnja datang
Aku tidak lagi meraih petang
Biar berleleran kata manis madu
Djika menagih jang satu

MY HOUSE

My house is built of heaped-up poems
Clear glass through which you can see everything

I ran away from the house, the big yard
I'm lost, I can't find the way

I pitched a tent in the twilight
By morning it had flown who knows where

My house is built of heaped-up poems
Here's where I married and had children

It feels like a long wait, but it will come
Now I don't grope for the afternoon, the evening
Let the honeyed words melt
If anyone comes to collect on them.

April 1943

HAMPA

Kepada Sri jang selalu sangsi

Sepi diluar. Sepi menekan-mendesak.
Lurus kaku pohonan. Tak bergerak
Sampai kepuntjak. Sepi memagut,
Tak satu kuasa melepas-renggut
Segala menanti. Menanti. Menanti
Sepi
Tambah ini menanti djadi mentjekik
Memberat-mentjengkung punda
Sampai binasa segala. Belum apa-apa
Udara bertuba. Setan bertempik
Ini sepi terus ada. Dan menanti.

EMPTY

to Sri, who always disbelieves

Quiet outside, quiet squeezes down
Stiff straight trees, motionless
Straight to the top.
Quiet snaps, gnaws,
No strength, no courage to run
Everything waits. Waits. Waits
Quiet.
And then this waiting strangles
Squeezes, bends
Till everything's crushed. So what.
The air is poisoned. The devil shrieks
This quiet goes on and on. And waits. Waits.

May 1943

KAWANKU DAN AKU

Kepada L.K.Bohang

Kami sama pedjalan larut
Menembus kabut
Hudjan mengutjur badan
Berkakuan kapal-kapal dipelabuhan

Darahku mengental pekat. Aku tumpat pedat

Siapa berkata-kata . . . . . . ?
Kawanku hanja rangka sadja
Karena dera mengelutjak tenaga

Dia bertanja djam berapa?

Sudah larut sekali
Hilang tenggelam segala makna
Dan gerak tak punja arti.

MY FRIEND AND I

to L.K.Bohang

We walk together, late,
Cutting the fog.
Rain soaks us.
Boats in the harbor freeze

My blood thickens and slows. My mind clots

Who's talking?
My friend is only a skeleton,
Whipped till the strength peels away

He asks, What time is it?

Too late.
Meaning has drowned
And motion makes no sense.

June 1943

BERTJERAI

Kita musti bertjerai
Sebelum kitjau murai berderai.

Terlalu kita minta pada malam ini.

Benar belum puas serah menjerah
Darah masih berbusah-busah.

Terlalu kita minta pada malam ini.

Kita musti bertjerai
Biar surja 'kan menembus oleh malam diperisai

Dua benua bakal bentur-membentur.
Merah kesumba djadi putih kapur.

Bagaimana?
Kau IDA, mau turut mengabur
Tidak samudra tjaja tempatmu menghambur.

PARTING

We've got to break this off
Before the morning birds begin to chirp.

We're asking for too much, tonight.

It's true, we haven't finished, there's more,
Our blood is still foaming.

We're asking for too much, tonight.

We've got to break this off
Let the sun that could stab through be hidden by night

Two half-formed continents are going to collide.
The one that's dark red will turn chalky white.

What?
You, IDA, you want to just fade away
There's no ocean for your glow to leap into.

June 1943

AKU

Melangkahkan aku bukan tuak menggelegak
Tjumbu-buatan satu biduan
Kudjauhi ahli agama serta lembing katanja.

Aku hidup
Dalam hidup dimata tampak bergerak
Dengan tjatjar melebar, barah bernanah
Dan kadang satu senjum kukutjup-minum dalam dahaga.

ME [Poem #2]

I don't move along like bubbling palm-wine
A crooner's phoney flattery
I keep away from psalm-singers and their so-called spears.

I live
In life at the center where it's moving
Where its pox gape, its boils fester
And now and then there's a single smile which I kiss
     and from which, in my thirst, I drink.

June 1943

TJERITA

Kepada Darmawidjaja

Dipasar baru mereka
Lalu mengada-menggaja.

Mengikat sudah kesal
Tak tahu apa dibuat

Djiwa satu teman lutju
Dalam hidup, dalam tudju.

Gundul diselimuti tebal
Sama segala berbuat-buat.

Tapi kadang pula dapat
Ini renggang terus terapat.

A STORY

To Darmawidjaja

The market: he tries to spin it
Out, boasting, lying.

It's spite talking.
He can't pull it off.

A clown:
Nothing else in mind.

A fog of bald words,
Always, in everything.

But that sort of gap
Is hard to paper over.

June 1943

DIMESDJID

Kuseru sadja Dia
Sehingga datang djuga

Kamipun bermuka-muka.

Seterusnja Ia bernjala-njala dalam dada.
Segala daja memadamkannja

Bersimpah peluh diri jang tak bisa diperkuda

Ini ruang
Gelanggang kami berperang

Binasa-membinasa
Satu menista lain gila.

AT THE MOSQUE

I shouted at Him
Until He came

We met face to face.

Afterwards He burned in my breast.
All my strength struggles to extinguish Him.

My body, which won't be driven, is soaked with sweat.

This
Is the arena where we fight

Destroying each other
One hurling insults, the other gone mad.

June 1943

KEPADA PEMINTA-MINTA

Baik, baik, aku akan menghadap Dia
Menjerahkan diri dan segala dosa
Tapi djangan tentang lagi aku
Nanti darahku djadi beku.

Djangan lagi kau bertjerita
Sudah tertjatjar semua dimuka
Nanah meleleh dari muka
Sambil berdjalan kau usap djuga.

Bersuara tiap kau melangkah
Mengerang tiap kau memandang
Menetes dari suasana kau datang
Sembarang kau merebah.

Mengganggu dalam mimpiku
Menghempas aku dibumi keras
Dibibirku terasa pedas
Mengaum ditelingaku.

Baik, baik, aku akan menghadap Dia
Menjerahkan diri dan segala dosa
Tapi djangan tentang lagi aku
Nanti darahku djadi beku.

TO A BEGGAR

All right, all right, I'll present myself to Him,
Surrender myself and all my sins,
But just stop staring at me
Or my blood will clot.

Don't tell that story anymore:
It's already been vaccinated all over your face,
Pus is trickling out of it,
You wipe it away as you walk.

You groan at every step,
Moan every time you focus your eyes,
Dripping with your sickness you come,
Flopping down wherever you fall.

Breaking into my dream
Throws me onto the hard ground,
I feel it biting at my lips,
Buzzing in my ears.

All right, all right, I'll present myself to Him,
Surrender myself and all my sins,
But just stop staring at me
Or my blood will clot.

June 1943

SELAMAT TINGGAL

"Perempuan . . . . . ."

Aku berkatja

Ini muka penuh luka
Siapa punja?

Kudengar seru menderu
—dalam hatiku?—
Apa hanja angin lalu?

Lagu lain pula
Menggelepar tengah malam buta

Ah . . . . . . ! ! !

Segala menebal, segala mengental
Segala tak kukenal
Selamat tinggal . . . . . . ! ! !

GOODBYE

"Woman . . . . . ."

My mirror: I see

This face covered with wounds:
Whose face?

I hear someone calling, crying
—in my heart?
—only the wind blowing by?

And then another song
Twitching in the blind-dark night

Ah . . . . . . ! ! !

Everything thickens, everything congeals
I don't know anything . . . . . .

Goodbye . . . . . . ! ! !

July 1943

Mulutmu mentjubit dimulutku
Menggelegak bentji sedjenak itu
Mengapa merihmu tak kutjekik pula
Ketika halus-perih kau meluka ? ?

YOUR MOUTH (title supplied)

Your mouth was nibbling at mine.
At that moment hatred boiled up in me.
Why didn't I strangle you
While you were gently hurting me?

July 1943

DENDAM

Berdiri tersentak
Dari mimpi aku bengis dielak

Aku tegak
Bulan bersinar sedikit tak nampak

Tangan meraba kebawah bantalku
Keris berkarat kugenggam dihulu

Bulan bersinar sedikit tak nampak

Aku mentjari
Mendadak mati kuhendak berbekas didjari

Aku mentjari
Diri tertjerai dari hati

Bulan bersinar sedikit tak nampak

REVENGE

I woke with a start
Pulled savagely out of my dream

I stood up
The moon hung dim

I fumbled under my pillow
I took the handle of my rusty dagger

The moon hung dim

I hunted
Suddenly my will could not reach my fingers

I hunted
Split away from myself

The moon hung dim

July 1943

MERDEKA

Aku mau bebas dari segala
Merdeka
Djuga dari Ida

Pernah
Aku pertjaja pada sumpah dan tjinta
Mendjadi sumsum dan darah
Seharian kukunjah—kumamah

Sedang meradang
Segala kurenggut
Ikut bajang

Tapi kini
Hidupku terlalu tenang
Selama tidak antara badai
Kalah menang

Ah! Djiwa jang menggapai-gapai
Mengapa kalau berandjak dari sini
Kutjoba dalam mati.

FREE

I want to be free of everything
Free
From Ida too

Once
I believed in promises, and in love,
Made them marrow and blood,
Chewed them all day long

Then in a fury
I ripped it all away
And chased after shadows

But now
My life's too calm
Out of the center of the storm
Away from victory or defeat

Ah! You clawing soul
If you're leaving here
Why can I taste you only in death?

July 1943

Kita gujah lemah
Sekali tetak tentu rebah
Segala erang dan djeritan
Kita pendam dalam keseharian

Mari tegak merentak
Diri-sekeliling kita bentak
Ini malam purnama akan menembus awan.

WE WOBBLE ALONG (title supplied)

We wobble along,
One whack and down we go,
All day long we hide
Our moaning and groaning

Why not stand straight, shove back,
Snarl:
Tonight the moon will break through the clouds.

July 1943 (?)

?

Djangan kita disini berhenti
Tuaknja tua, sedikit pula
Sedang kita mau berkendi-kendi
Terus, terus dulu . . . . . . ! ! !

Keruang dimana botol tuak banjak berbaris
Pelajannja kita dilajani gadis-gadis
O, bibir merah, selokan mati pertama
O, hidup, kau masih ketawa ? ?

?

Let's not stop here
The beer is stale, and scarce at that
And we want barrels and barrels
Go on, let's go on . . . . . . ! ! !

Off to a place where the bottles stand in rows
And it's girls who bring it to us
Oh red lips, the first of death's sewers
Oh life, are you still laughing ? ?

July 1943

1943

Ratjun berada direguk pertama
Membusuk rabu terasa didada
Tenggelam darah dalam nanah
Malam kelam-membelam
Djalan kaku-lurus. Putus
Tjandu.
Tumbang
Tanganku menadah patah
Luluh
Terbenam
Hilang
Lumpuh.
Lahir
Tegak
Berderak
Rubuh
Runtuh
Mengaum. Mengguruh
Menentang. Menjerang
Kuning
Merah
Hitam
Kering
Tandas
Rata
Rata
Rata
Dunia
Kau
Aku
Terpaku.

1943

There's poison in the first slug of it
It stinks as it goes into you
Blood drowning in pus
The evening pitch-black
The roads stiff-straight. The opium
Used up.
Collapsing
My hands catch brokenly
Smashed
Drowned
Lost
Paralyzed.
I am born
Stand
Creak
Fall
In a heap
Roaring. Thundering
Challenging. Attacking
Yellow
Red
Black
Arid
Exhausted
Flat
Flat
Flat
Is the world
You
And me
Nailed down.

1943

ISA

Kepada Nasrani Sedjati

Itu Tubuh
mengutjur darah
mengutjur darah

rubuh
patah

mendampar tanja: aku salah?

kulihat Tubuh mengutjur darah
aku berkatja dalam darah

terbajang terang dimata masa
bertukar rupa ini segara

mengatup luka

aku bersuka

Itu Tubuh
mengutjur darah
mengutjur darah

JESUS CHRIST

to the true Christian

This Body
Bleeding
Bleeding

Fallen
Broken

Floats up a question: am I to blame?

I see that bleeding Body
And what I see in that blood is: me

Reflected brightly in the eye of time
This will change form, soon

Close its wounds

I am glad

This Body
Bleeding
Bleeding

November 1943

DOA

Kepada Pemeluk Teguh

Tuhanku
Dalam termangu
Aku masih menjebut namaMu

Biar susah sungguh
mengingat Kau penuh seluruh

tjajaMu panas sutji
tinggal kerdip lilin dikelam sunji

Tuhanku

aku hilang bentuk
remuk

Tuhanku

aku mengembara dinegeri asing

Tuhanku
dipintuMu aku mengetuk
aku tidak bisa berpaling

PRAYER

to the faithful

My God
When my soul is reeling
I still call Your name

Though it's hard, hard
To really remember You

Your warm pure light
Remains a flickering candle in the lonely dark

My God

I've lost all form
Shattered

My God

I wander in strange lands

My God
I knock at Your door
I cannot turn away

November 1943

SADJAK PUTIH

buat tunanganku Mirat

Bersandar pada tari warna pelangi
Kau depanku bertudung sutra sendja
Dihitam matamu kembang mawar dan melati
Harum rambutmu mengalun bergelut senda

Sepi menjanji, malam dalam mendoa tiba
Meriak muka air kolam djiwa
Dan dalam dadaku memerdu lagu
Menarik menari seluruh aku

Hidup dari hidupku, pintu terbuka
Selama matamu bagiku menengadah

Selama kau darah mengalir dari luka
Antara kita Mati datang tidak membelah . . . . . .

A PURE RHYME

for Mirat, my fiancée

Leaning into a rainbow-colored dance
In front of me, veiled in dusky silk
Roses and jasmine in your black eyes
The fragrance of your hair teasing, swelling

Singing of loneliness, in prayer, the night comes,
The waters of the soul stir,
And in my breast an enchanting song
Pulls all of me into the dance

Live from my life, the door is open
As long as your eyes look up at me

As long as my blood spills on
Death will never come between us . . . . . .

January 1944

DALAM KERETA

Dalam kereta.
Hudjan menebal djendela.

Semarang, Solo . . . . . . , makin dekat sadja
Menangkup sendja.

Menguak purnama.
Tjaja menjajat mulut dan mata.
Mendjengking kereta. Mendjengking djiwa.

Sajatan terus kedada.

IN THE TRAIN

In the train.
Rain thickens on the window.

Semarang, Solo . . . . . . , coming closer,
Twilight closes down.

The moon springs out.
Its rays slit mouths and eyes.
Overturn the train. Overturn souls.

Slicing clear through the breast.

March 1944

SIAP-SEDIA

Kepada Angkatanku

Tanganmu nanti tegang kaku,
Djantungmu nanti berdebar berhenti,
Tubuhmu nanti mengeras batu,
Tapi kami sederap mengganti,
Terus memahat ini Tugu.

Matamu nanti katja sadja,
Mulutmu nanti habis bitjara,
Darahmu nanti mengalir berhenti,
Tapi kami sederap mengganti,
Terus berdaja ke Masjarakat Djaja.

Suaramu nanti diam ditekan,
Namamu nanti terbang hilang,
Langkahmu nanti enggan kedepan,
Tapi kami sederap mengganti,
Bersatu madju, ke Kemenangan.

Darah kami panas selama,
Badan kami tertempa badja,
Djiwa kami gagah perkasa,
Kami akan mewarna diangkasa,
Kami pembawa ke Bahgia njata.

Kawan, kawan
Menepis segar angin terasa
Lalu menderu menjapu awan
Terus menembus surja tjahaja

WE'RE READY

to my generation

By then your hands will be stiff,
By then your heart will have stopped beating,
By then your body will have turned to stone,
But we'll quickly find others,
We'll go on carving this Monument.

By then your eyes will be only glass,
By then your mouth will have forgotten speech,
By then your blood will have stopped pounding,
But we'll quickly find others,
We'll push on to a World of Triumph.

By then your voice will be stifled,
By then your name will have vanished,
By then you won't want to march forward,
But we'll quickly find others,
Advancing together, to Victory.

Our blood is forever warm,
Our bodies are forged of steel,
Our spirit is strong, is brave,
We'll repaint the skies,
We're the bearers of real happiness.

Friends, my friends,
How skimming fresh the wind
Howling as it wipes away clouds,
Shoving the sun on through

Memantjar pentjar kependjuru segala
Riang menggelombang sawah dan hutan

Segala menjala-njala!
Segala menjala-njala!

Kawan, kawan
Dan kita bangkit dengan kesedaran
Mentjutjuk menerang hingga belulang.
Kawan, kawan
Kita mengajun pedang ke Dunia Terang!

Pouring light into every corner.
Fields and woods shake and bend with pleasure.

Everything's burning!
Everything's burning!

Friends, oh friends,
Let's rise up knowingly
Stabbing the new light deep under the skin.
Friends, friends,
Let's swing our swords toward the Bright World!

1944

KEPADA PENJAIR BOHANG

Suaramu bertanda derita laut tenang . . . . . .
Si Mati ini padaku masih berbitjara
Karena dia tjinta, dimulutnja membusah
Dan rindu jang mau memerahi segala
Si Mati ini matanja terus bertanja!

Kelana tidak bersedjarah
Berdjalan kau terus!
Sehingga tidak gelisah
Begitu berlumuran darah.

Dan duka djuga menengadah
Melihat gajamu melangkah
Mendaju suara patah:
'Aku saksi!'

Bohang,
Djauh didasar djiwamu
bertampuk suatu dunia;
mengujup rintik satu-satu
Katja dari dirimu pula . . . . . .

FOR THE POET BOHANG

Your voice has the sorrow of the still ocean . . . . . .
This Corpse still speaks to me.
Because he loved, his mouth foams
With a longing that wants to squeeze out everything.
This Corpse, his eyes go on asking!

Wanderer without history
Walk on!
Until it means nothing to you
That you're splattered with blood.

And sorrow too lifts its head
Seeing the strength in your stride,
Moaning in its broken voice:
"I am a witness!"

Bohang,
A world of faith
Blossoms in the depths of your soul;
The drops soak down one by one.
And your image is reflected, too . . . . . .

1945

LAGU SIUL

I

Laron pada mati
Terbakar disumbu lampu
Aku djuga menemu
Adjal ditjerlang tjaja matamu
Heran! ini badan jang selama berdjaga
Habis hangus diapi matamu
'Ku kajak tidak tahu sadja.

II

Aku kira
Beginilah nanti djadinja:
Kau kawin, beranak dan berbahagia
Sedang aku mengembara serupa Ahasveros

Dikutuk-sumpahi Eros
Aku merangkaki dinding buta,
Tak satu djuga pintu terbuka.

Djadi baik kita padami
Unggunan api ini
Karena kau tidak 'kan apa-apa,
Aku terpanggang tinggal rangka.

WHISTLING SONG

I

The moths are all dead
Burned in the lamp wick
Just as I meet my final agony
In the light of your bright eyes
Fantastic! This body forever on guard
Is charred to a crisp by the flame of your eyes
I seem to know nothing.

II

I think
This will be the end of it:
You'll marry, have children and happiness
While I wander like Ahasuerus.

Cursed by Eros
I crawl the blank walls,
But no door opens.

We were right to snuff out
This brush-fire
Because you won't care and
I will be left a roasted skeleton.

November 1945 and February 1943

MALAM

Mulai kelam
belum buntu malam,
kami masih sadja berdjaga
——Thermopylae?—
—djagal tidak dikenal?—
tapi nanti
sebelum siang membentang
kami sudah tenggelam
hilang . . . . . .

EVENING

It begins to darken
But not yet into that dead-end
Which is night;
We're still only
      watching, waiting
——for Thermopylae?——
—an unknown Butcher?—
Yet later
Before the day-light spreads out
We'll have sunk down
      away . . . . . .

1945

ORANG BERDUA

Kamar ini djadi sarang penghabisan
dimalam jang hilang batas

Aku dan dia hanja mendjengkau
rakit hitam

Kan terdamparkah
atau terserah
pada putaran pitam?

Matamu ungu membatu

Masih berdekapankah kami atau
mengikut djuga bajangan itu?

TOGETHER

This room becomes our final nest
In an endless night

She and I, we only reach out for
The black raft

Will we be washed ashore
Or let ourselves whirl
In dizzy circles?

Your eyes are like violet stones

Are we still embracing or
Just aping that shadow?

January 1946

SEBUAH KAMAR

Sebuah djendela menjerahkan kamar ini
pada dunia. Bulan jang menjinar kedalam
mau lebih banjak tahu.
'Sudah lima anak bernjawa disini,
Aku salah satu!'

Ibuku tertidur dalam tersedu,
Keramaian pendjara sepi selalu,
Bapakku sendiri terbaring djemu
Matanja menatap orang tersalib dibatu!

Sekeliling dunia bunuh diri!
Aku minta adik lagi pada
Ibu dan bapakku, karena mereka berada
diluar hitungan: Kamar begini,
3 x 4 m, terlalu sempit buat meniup njawa!

A ROOM

A window surrenders this room
To the world. The moon that shines in
Wants to know a lot more.
"Five children live here, five!
And I'm one of them!"

My mother falls asleep, sobbing,
Prison crowds are always lonely,
Even my father stretches out, bored,
His eyes fixed on the carved-stone crucifix!

The whole world is committing suicide!
I beg for another younger brother from
My mother and father, since they're not included
In the count: A room like this,
3 yards by 4, is too tight a fit for playing at life!

1946

KEPADA PELUKIS AFFANDI

Kalau, 'ku habis-habis kata, tidak lagi
berani memasuki rumah sendiri, terdiri
diambang penuh kupak,

adalah karena kesementaraan segala
jang mentjap tiap benda, lagi pula terasa
mati kan datang merusak.

Dan tangan 'kan kaku, menulis berhenti,
ketjemasan derita, ketjemasan mimpi;
berilah aku tempat dimenara tinggi,
dimana kau sendiri meninggi

atas keramaian dunia dan tjedera,
lagak lahir dan kelantjungan tjipta,
kau memaling dan memudja
dan gelap-tertutup djadi terbuka!

TO THE PAINTER AFFANDI

If I have run out of words, no longer
Dare to enter my own house, standing
On the crumbling doorstep,

The reason is the eternal transience
Stamped into every piece of every thing, and even more
The sense of death coming, destroying.

And hands will stiffen, will no longer write,
Troubled by pain, troubled by dreams.
Give me a place on a lofty tower
Where you alone rise over

Crowds and noise and betrayal,
Over easy pretence and make-believe creation,
Where you turn away, you pray,
And the closed-up darkness opens!

1946

TJATETAN TH. 1946

Ada tanganku, sekali akan djemu terkulai,
Mainan tjahja diair hilang bentuk dalam kabut,
Dan suara jang kutjintai 'kan berhenti membelai.
Kupahat batu nisan sendiri dan kupagut.

Kita—andjing diburu—hanja melihat sebagian dari sandiwara
    sekarang
Tidak tahu Romeo & Juliet berpeluk dikubur atau dirandjang
Lahir seorang besar dan tenggelam beratus ribu
Keduanja harus ditjatet, keduanja dapat tempat.

Dan kita nanti tiada sawan lagi diburu
Djika bedil sudah disimpan, tjuma kenangan berdebu,
Kita memburu arti atau diserahkan pada anak lahir sempat,
Karena itu djangan mengerdip, tatap dan penamu asah,
Tulis karena kertas gersang, tenggorokan kering sedikit mau
    basah!

NOTES FOR 1946

These hands, which some day will sag with disgust,
These hands flick brightly through water,
These hands lose all shape in thick mist,
And the voice I love will not caress me.
I cut a grave-stone and peck away at it.

We—running dogs, hunting hounds—we get to see
Only a moment of this drama we play in,
Unaware of Romeo & Juliet wound in each other's arms
In their tomb or in their bed—
Of a great man born, of hundreds drowned,
All of which must be noted, all of which has a place.

And then, in the end, the shaking-sickness will hunt us no longer
If the hunting gun is stored away,
If the hunting gun is no more than a dusty souvenir.
We hunt hard after Meaning—or we submit like lazy,
    sophisticated children.
So don't blink—watch, stare, sharpen your pen,
Write because the page is empty,
Because when the throat starts to go dry it wants water!

1946

BUAT ALBUM D.S.

Seorang gadis lagi menjanji
Lagu derita dipantai jang djauh,
Kelasi bersendiri dilaut biru, dari
Mereka jang sudah lupa bersuka.

Suaranja pergi terus meninggi,
Kami jang mendengar melihat sendja
Mentjium belai sigadis pada pipi
Dan gaum putihnja sebagian dari mimpi.

Kami rasa bahgia tentu 'kan tiba,
Kelasi mendapat dekapan dipelabuhan
Dan dinegeri kelabu jang berhiba
Penduduknja bersinar lagi, dapat tudjuan

Lagu merdu!—apa mengertikah adikku ketjil
jang menangis mengiris hati
Bahwa pelarian akan terus tinggal terpentjil,
Djuga dinegeri djauh itu surja tidak kembali?

D.S.: FOR HER ALBUM

A girl is singing
A sad song on a far-away shore,
A sailor is lonely on the blue sea, because
Of those who forgot to be happy.

Her voice goes higher and higher,
We who listen watch the twilight
Kiss and caress her cheek
And her white dress, like something in a dream.

We're sure that happiness will come,
The sailor will be embraced at the harbor
And in that sad, grey country
People will rejoice, finding the True Way.

A marvellous song!—But do you understand,
My sadly sobbing little sister,
That a deserter will always be deserted,
And that even in that far country the sun never goes backward?

1946

95

NOCTURNO (FRAGMENT)

. . . .
Aku menjeru—tapi tidak satu suara
membalas, hanja mati dibeku udara.
Dalam diriku terbudjar keinginan,
djuga tidak bernjawa.
Mimpi jang penghabisan minta tenaga,
Patah kapak, sia-sia berdaja,
Dalam tjekikan hatiku

Terdampar . . . . . . Menginjam abu dan debu
Dari tinggalnja suatu lagu.
Ingatan pada Adjal jang menghantu.
Dan demam jang nanti membikin kaku . . . . . .

. . . .
Pena dan penjair keduanja mati,
Berpalingan!

NOCTURNO: A FRAGMENT

I shouted—but no voice answered,
My cry died in the frozen air: died.
Desires stretched in me too,
Also dead.
The last dream begged for strength,
The axe broke, swung hard, in vain,
And my heart strangled.

Stranded . . . . . . I taste ashes and dust
From a left-over song.
A whiff of that haunted Emptiness
And the fever that will stiffen me . . . . . .

. . . .
Pen and poet, both dead,
Turning!

1946

TJERITA BUAT DIEN TAMAELA

Beta Pattiradjawane
Jang didjaga datu-datu
Tjuma satu.

Beta Pattiradjawane
Kikisan laut.
Berdarah laut.

Beta Pattiradjawane
Ketika lahir dibawakan
Datu dajung sampan.

Beta Pattiradjawane, mendjaga hutan pala.
Beta api dipantai. Siapa mendekat
Tiga kali menjebut punja nama.

Dalam sunji malam ganggang menari
Menurut beta punja tifa,
Pohon pala, badan perawan djadi
Hidup sampai pagi tiba.

Mari menari!
mari beria!
mari berlupa!

Awas djangan bikin beta marah
Beta bikin pala mati, gadis kaku
Beta kirim datu-datu!

A TALE FOR DIEN TAMAELA

I am Pattiradjawane
Whom the gods watch over
I alone.

I am Pattiradjawane
Foam of the sea.
The sea is my blood.

I am Pattiradjawane
When I was born
The gods brought me an oar.

I am Pattiradjawane, guarding the nutmeg groves.
I am fire on the shore. Whoever comes near
Must call my name three times.

In the night-time quiet, seaweed dances
To the sound of my drum,
Nutmeg trees become maidens' bodies
And live till dawn.

Dance!
Be happy!
Forget everything!

But take care not to make me angry
I'll kill the nut trees, stiffen the maidens
I'll bring down the gods!

Beta ada dimalam, ada disiang
Irama ganggang dan api membakar pulau . . . . . .

Beta Pattiradjawane
Jang didjaga datu-datu
Tjuma satu.

I'm in the night, in the day,
In the rhythm of the seaweed and in the fire
    that roasts the island . . . . . .

I am Pattiradjawane
Whom the gods watch over
I alone.

1946

KABAR DARI LAUT

Aku memang benar tolol ketika itu,
mau pula membikin hubungan dengan kau;
lupa kelasi tiba-tiba bisa sendiri dilaut pilu,
berudjuk kembali dengan tudjuan biru.

Ditubuhku ada luka sekarang,
bertambah lebar djuga, mengeluar darah,
dibekas dulu kau tjium napsu dan garang;
lagi akupun sangat lemah serta menjerah.

Hidup berlangsung antara buritan dan kemudi.
Pembatasan tjuma tambah menjatukan kenang.
Dan tawa gila pada whisky tertjermin tenang.

Dan kau? Apakah kerdjamu sembahjang dan memudji,
Atau diantara mereka djuga terdampar,
Burung mati pagi hari disisi sangkar?

NEWS FROM THE SEA

I was really a fool that time,
Wanting to sleep with you,
Forgetting how quickly a sailor can find himself alone
       on the sad sea,
Reconciled to his blue destination.

Now there's a wound on my body,
Widening, spilling out blood from
The place where you kissed me, then, with a fierce lust
And I was far too weak, and surrendered.

Life goes on between the stern and the ship's wheel.
Definitions only strengthen memory.
And crazy laughter is reflected in the quiet whisky.

And you? Is your job prayer and praise,
Or is there something washed up between them,
A bird that, at dawn, is dead against the bars of its cage?

1946

SENDJA DI PELABUHAN KETJIL

Buat Sri Ajati

Ini kali tidak ada jang mentjari tjinta
diantara gudang, rumah tua, pada tjerita
tiang serta temali. Kapal, perahu tidak berlaut
menghembus diri dalam mempertjaja mau berpaut

Gerimis mempertjepat kelam. Ada djuga kelepak elang
menjinggung muram, desir hari lari berenang
menemu budjuk pangkal akanan. Tidak bergerak
dan kini tanah dan air tidur hilang ombak.

Tiada lagi. Aku sendiri. Berdjalan
menjisir semenandjung, masih pengap harap
sekali tiba diudjung dan sekalian selamat djalan
dari pantai keempat, sedu penghabisan bisa terdekap.

TWILIGHT AT A LITTLE HARBOR

for Sri Ajati

This time no one's looking for love
Between the sheds, the old houses, in the twitter
Of poles and rigging. A boat, a *prau* forever out of water
Puffs and snorts, thinking there's something it can catch hold of

The drizzle brings down darkness. There's an eagle flapping;
With a flick, the day brushes at the gloom, then swims silkily
To meet temptations yet to come. Nothing moves.
And now the sand and the sea are asleep, the waves are gone.

That's all. I'm alone. Walking,
Combing the cape, still drowning the hope
Of getting to the end of it and just once saying goodbye
    to everything
From the fourth beach, embracing the last, the final sob of all.

1946

TJINTAKU DJAUH DIPULAU

Tjintaku djauh dipulau,
gadis manis, sekarang iseng sendiri.

Perahu melantjar, bulan memantjar,
dileher kukalungkan ole-ole buat sipatjar,
angin membantu, laut terang, tapi terasa
aku tidak 'kan sampai padanja.

Diair jang tenang, diangin mendaju,
diperasaan penghabisan segala meladju
Adjal bertachta, sambil berkata:
'Tudjukan perahu kepangkuanku sadja.'

Amboi! Djalan sudah bertahun kutempuh!
Perahu jang bersama 'kan merapuh!
Mengapa Adjal memanggil dulu
Sebelum sempat berpeluk dengan tjintaku?!

Manisku djauh dipulau,
kalau 'ku mati, dia mati iseng sendiri.

MY LOVE'S ON A FARAWAY ISLAND

My love's on a faraway island,
A sweet girl, doing nothing for lack of anything better.

The *prau* slides quickly along, the moon gleams,
Around my neck I wear a charm for my girl;
The wind helps, the sea's clear, but I know
I'm not going to reach her.

In the calm water, in the gentle wind,
In the final sensation, everything goes swiftly.
Death pulls the strings, calls:
"Better steer your *prau* straight into my lap."

Hey! I've made it through this way for years!
This *prau* of mine is going to fall apart!
Why is Death calling so soon
Before I have a chance to hug my girl?!

My sweet on a faraway island,
If I die, she'll die for lack of anything better.

1946

"BETINA"–NJA AFFANDI

Betina, djika dibarat nanti
mendjadi gelap
turut tenggelam sama sekali
djuga jang mengendap,
dimukamu tinggal bermain Hidup dan Mati.

Matamu menentang—sebentar dulu!—
Kau tidak gamang, hidup kau sintuh, kau tjumbu,
sekarang sendja gosong, tinggal abu . . . . . .
Dalam tubuhmu ramping masih bekedjaran Perempuan dan Laki.

AFFANDI'S SLUT

Female, if after a while
It darkens to the west,
Sinks down
To the last dregs,
Life and Death still play across your face.

Your eyes say: to hell with you—just a minute!—
You're not afraid, you finger life, you flatter, you tease it,
Now that the twilight has burned itself to ashes . . . . . .
In your slender body, Man and Woman still chase each other,
      around and around.

1946

SITUASI

. . . .
Tidak perempuan! Jang hidup dalam diri
masih lintjah mengelak dari pelukanmu gemas gelap,
bersikeras mentjari kehidjauan laut lain,
dan berada lagi dikapal dulu bertemu,
berlepas kemudi pada angin,
mata terpikat pada bintang jang menanti.
Sesuatu jang mengepak kembali menandungkan
Tai Po dan rahsia laut Ambon
Begitulah perempuan! Hanja suatu garis kabur
bisa dituliskan
dengan pelarian kebuntuan senjuman.

SITUATION

No, woman! What lives in me
Still dodges away from your sour, dark embrace,
Hunting as hard as it knows for the green of some other sea
And that ship where we first met,
Letting the wind be the steersman,
Eyes glued on a waiting star.
Something that was flapping its wings goes back to prating
About Tu Fu and the secret of the Ambon Sea.
And that's that, woman! All I can write
Is a single blurred line
In my race to that unresolvable smile.

1946

DARI DIA

Buat K.

Djangan salahkan aku, kau kudekap
bukan karena setia, lalu pergi gemerentjing ketawa!
Sebab perempuan susah mengatasi
keterharuan penghidupan jang 'kan dibawakan
padanja . . . . . .

Sebut namaku! 'ku datang kembali kekamar
Jang kau tandai lampu merah, cactus didjendela,
Tidak tahu buat berapa lama, tapi pasti disendja samar
Rambutku ikal menjinar, kau senapsu dulu kuhela

Sementara biarkan 'ku hidup jang sudah
didjalinkan dalam rahsia . . . . . .

FROM HER

For K.

Why blame me—I'm not embracing you
Because I'm faithful—I'll leave you afterwards with
    a ringing laugh!
It isn't easy for a woman to escape
Emotions as life brings them
To her . . . . . .

Call my name! I'll come back to the room
You've marked with a red lamp and a cactus in the window;
I don't know for how long, but I do know that in the vague dusk
My wavy hair will shine, and you'll be as passionate as you were
    the last time I drew you to me

And in the meantime let me be, in this life
Woven in secret . . . . . .

1946

KEPADA KAWAN

Sebelum adjal mendekat dan mengchianat,
mentjengkam dari belakang 'tika kita tidak melihat,
selama masih menggelombang dalam dada darah serta rasa,

belum bertunas ketjewa dan gentar belum ada,
tidak lupa tiba-tiba bisa malam membenam,
lajar merah terkibar hilang dalam kelam,
kawan, mari kita putuskan kini disini:
Adjal jang menarik kita, djuga mentjekik diri sendiri!

Djadi
Isi gelas sepenuhnja lantas kosongkan,
Tembus djeladjah dunia ini dan balikkan,
Peluk kutjup perempuan, tinggalkan kalau meraju,
Pilih kuda jang paling liar, patju ladju,
Djangan tambatkan pada siang dan malam
Dan
Hantjurkan lagi apa jang kau perbuat,
Hilang sonder pusaka, sonder kerabat,
Tidak minta ampun atas segala dosa,
Tidak memberi pamit pada siapa sadja!

Djadi
mari kita putuskan sekali lagi:
Adjal jang menarik kita, 'kan merasa angkasa sepi,
Sekali lagi kawan, sebaris lagi·
Tikamkan pedangmu hingga kehulu
Pada siapa jang mengairi kemurnian madu ! ! !

TO A FRIEND

Before Death draws closer, and betrayal,
Leaping at us from behind when we're looking the other way,
While blood still beats in our hearts and we still have feeling,

And despair has not bloomed and there is no fear,
Remember how quickly the evening can fade, without warning,
A red sail fluttering down in the darkness,
And, friend, let's part now, here:
This Death which pulls at us also strangles itself!

So
If there's a full glass, empty it,
Pierce, explore the world, turn it upside down,
Love women, but leave the flatterers and the sad ones,
Rope the wildest horse, spur him swiftly,
Tie him to neither noon nor night
And
Smash whatever you've made,
End without inheritance, without family,
Without requesting forgiveness for all your sins,
Without a farewell to anyone!

So
Again
Let us part:
This Death which pulls at us will find the sky lonely—deserted.
Once more, friend, one line more:
Shove your sword to the hilt
Into those who've diluted the pureness of honey ! ! !

November 1946

115

PEMBERIAN TAHU

Bukan maksudku mau berbagi nasib,
nasib adalah kesunjian masing-masing.
Kupilih kau dari jang banjak, tapi
sebentar kita sudah dalam sepi lagi terdjaring.
Aku pernah ingin benar padamu,
Dimalam raja, mendjadi kanak-kanak kembali,
Kita berpeluk tjiuman tidak djemu,
Rasa tak sanggup kau kulepaskan.
Djangan satukan hidupmu dengan hidupku,
Aku memang tidak bisa lama bersama
Ini djuga kutulis dikapal, dilaut tidak bernama!

A PROCLAMATION

I don't intend to share fate,
Fate which is a universal loneliness.
I chose you out of the lot of them, but
It won't be long before we're tangled in loneliness again.
Once I really wanted you:
In the vast night, becoming little children again,
We kissed and clung and were never bored,
I felt I could never let you go.
Don't tie your life to mine,
I can't be with anyone for long.
And this, too, I'm writing on board ship,
From the sea that has no name!

1946

SADJAK BUAT BASUKI RESOBOWO

Adakah djauh perdjalanan ini?
Tjuma selenggang!—Tjoba kalau bisa lebih!
Lantas bagaimana?
Pada daun gugur tanja sendiri,
Dan sama lagu melembut djadi melodi!

Apa tinggal djadi tanda mata?
Lihat pada betina tidak lagi menengadah
Atau baju saju, bintang menghilang!

Lagi djalan ini berapa lama?
Boleh seabad . . . aduh sekerdip sadja!
Perdjalanan karna apa?
Tanja rumah asal jang bisu!
Keturunanku jang beku disitu!

Ada jang menggamit?
Ada jang kehilangan?
Ah! djawab sendiri!—Aku terus gelandangan . . . . . .

POEM FOR BASUKI RESOBOWO

Is this much of a journey?
Only a step!—Maybe *you* can go further!
But how?
Ask the fallen leaves for yourself,
Ask the quiet chant that becomes a song!

What stays behind to be remembered?
Look at those hens with their eyes lowered,
Or sad-faced slaves, or falling stars!

How long a journey?
Maybe a century . . . . . . no, no, just a wink of the eye!
But *why* this journey?
Ask the house, that was born dumb!
Ask my children's children, freezing in there!

Is something reaching out?
Is something letting go?
Ah, find your own answers!—I'm just killing time . . . . . .

February 1947

SORGA

Buat Basuki Resobowo

Seperti ibu + nenekku djuga
tambah tudjuh keturunan jang lalu
aku minta pula supaja sampai disorga
jang kata Masjumi + Muhammadijah bersungai susu
dan bertabur bidari beribu

Tapi ada suara menimbang dalam diriku,
nekat mentjemooh: Bisakah kiranja
berkering dari kujup laut biru,
gamitan dari tiap pelabuhan gimana?
Lagi siapa bisa mengatakan pasti
disitu memang ada bidari
suaranja berat menelan seperti Nina, punja kerlingnja Jati?

HEAVEN

for Basuki Resobowo

Like my mother, and my grandmother too,
Plus seven generations before them,
I also seek admission to heaven
Which the Moslem Party and the Mohammedan Union
      say has rivers of milk
And thousands of houris all over.

But there's a contemplative voice inside me,
Stubbornly mocking: Can you expect to
Get dry by soaking in the blue sea,
And what about the sly temptations waiting in every port?
Anyway, who can say for sure
That there really are houris there
With voices as rich and husky as Nina's, with eyes
      that flirt like Jati's?

February 1947

MALAM DI PEGUNUNGAN

Aku berpikir: Bulan inikah jang membikin dingin,
Djadi putjat rumah dan kaku pohonan?
Sekali ini aku terlalu sangat dapat djawab kepingin:
Eh, ada botjah tjilik main kedjaran dengan bajangan!

EVENING IN THE MOUNTAINS

I think: Is it the moon that's freezing everything,
Turning the houses white, stiffening the trees?
This time I really, really want an answer:
Hah—little boys are playing tag in the shadows!

1947

TUTI ARTIC

Antara bahagia sekarang dan nanti djurang ternganga,
Adikku jang lagi keenakan mendjilat es artic;
Sore ini kau tjintaku, kuhiasi dengan sus + coca cola.
Isteriku dalam latihan: kita hentikan djam berdetik.

Kau pintar benar bertjium, ada goresan tinggal terasa
—ketika kita bersepeda kuantar kau pulang—
Panas darahmu, sungguh lekas kau djadi dara,
Mimpi tua bangka kelangit lagi mendjulang.

Pilihanmu saban hari mendjemput, saban kali bertukar;
Besok kita berselisih djalan, tidak kenal tahu:
Sorga hanja permainan sebentar.

Aku djuga seperti kau, semua lekas berlalu
Aku dan Tuti + Greet + Amoi . . . . . . hati terlantar,
Tjinta adalah bahaja jang lekas djadi pudar.

TUTI'S ICE CREAM

Between present and future happiness
The abyss gapes.
My girl is licking happily at her ice cream:
This afternoon you're my love,
I adorn you with cake and coca-cola.
Oh wife-in-training, we have stopped the clocks' ticking.

You kissed skilfully, indelibly
—When we cycled I took you home
—Your blood was hot, oh you were a woman soon,
And the stiff old man dreamed dreams that leaped at the moon.

Every day's beau invited you on, every day's beau was different.
Tomorrow we'll meet in the street and not know each other:
Heaven is this minute's game.

I am like you, everything ran by,
Me and Tuti and Hreyt and Amoy . . . . . . dilapidated hearts.
Love's a danger that quickly fades.

1947

KRAWANG-BEKASI

Kami jang kini terbaring antara Krawang-Bekasi
tidak bisa teriak "Merdeka" dan angkat sendjata lagi.

Tapi siapakah jang tidak lagi mendengar deru kami,
terbajang kami madju dan berdegap hati?

Kami bitjara padamu dalam hening dimalam sepi
Djika dada rasa hampa dan djam dinding jang berdetak

Kami mati muda. Jang tinggal tulang diliputi debu.
Kenang, kenanglah kami.

Kami sudah tjoba apa jang kami bisa
Tapi kerdja belum selesai, belum apa-apa

Kami sudah beri kami punja djiwa
Kerdja belum selesai, belum bisa memperhitungkan arti 4-5 rib
        njawa

Kami tjuma tulang-tulang berserakan
Tapi adalah kepunjaanmu
Kaulah lagi jang tentukan nilai tulang-tulang berserakan
Ataukah djiwa kami melajang untuk kemerdekaan kemenangan
        dan harapan

atau tidak untuk apa-apa,
Kami tidak tahu, kami tidak lagi bisa berkata
Kaulah sekarang jang berkata

KRAWANG-BEKASI

We who are lying, now, near Krawang-Bekasi,
We can no longer cry out "Freedom," no longer lift our rifles

But who cannot still hear our moans?
Still see us marching forward, unafraid?

We speak to you out of the suspended silence of evening
When the chest feels empty, when clocks tick away time

We died young. All that remains of us: bones covered with dust.
Remember, remember us!

We've tried, done all we could
But the job isn't finished, is hardly begun

We've given the lives we had
The job isn't finished, no one can count up, still, the meaning of four
    thousand, of five thousand lives

We are only scattered bones
But they belong to you
And you will decide the value of these scattered bones

Either we died for freedom, for victory, for hope

Or for nothing.
We don't know, we can no longer say
Only you can speak, now

Kami bitjara padamu dalam hening dimalam sepi
Djika dada rasa hampa dan djam dinding jang berdetak

Kenang, kenanglah kami
Teruskan, teruskanlah djiwa kami
Mendjaga Bung Karno
Mendjaga Bung Hatta
Mendjaga Bung Sjahrir

Kami sekarang majat
Berilah kami arti
Berdjagalah terus digaris batas pernjataan dan impian

Kenang, kenanglah kami
jang tinggal tulang-tulang diliputi debu
Beribu kami terbaring antara Krawang-Bekasi.

We speak to you out of the suspended silence of evening
When the chest feels empty, when clocks tick away time

Remember, remember us—
Let our lives live on
Guarding Soekarno
Guarding Hatta
Guarding Sjahrir *

We are corpses
Give us meaning
Keep watch over the frontier between reality and illusion

Remember, remember us
Who survive only in these bones covered with dust
Thousands of us, lying near Krawang-Bekasi.

1948

* *Former President Soekarno, Former Vice President Hatta,*
  Former Socialist Party leader Sjahrir.

PERSETUDJUAN DENGAN BUNG KARNO

Ajo! Bung Karno kasi tangan mari kita bikin djandji
Aku sudah tjukup lama dengan bitjaramu, dipanggang atas
apimu, digarami oleh lautmu

Dari mula tgl. 17 Agustus 1945
Aku melangkah kedepan berada rapat disisimu
Aku sekarang api aku sekarang laut

Bung Karno! Kau dan aku satu zat satu urat
Dizatmu dizatku kapal-kapal kita berlajar
Diuratmu diuratku kapal-kapal kita berlajar
Diuratmu diuratku kapal-kapal kita bertolak & berlabuh

AGREEMENT WITH FRIEND SOEKARNO

Come on! Friend Soekarno, give me your hand, let's make a deal
I've heard enough of your speeches, been roasted by your
passion, salted by the sea-flood of you

From the day this country set itself free
I've marched along up front, right next to you
Now I'm on fire, now I'm flooding over

Friend Soekarno! You and me, we're cut from the same plug, we've
got the same guts
Our ships sail in your plug and in my plug
Our ships sail in your guts and in my guts
Our ships pull up and drop anchor in your guts and in my guts too.

1948

Sudah dulu lagi terdjadi begini
Djari tidak bakal terandjak dari petikan bedil
Djangan tanja mengapa djari tjari tempat disini
Aku tidak tahu tanggal serta alasan lagi
Dan djangan tanja siapa akan menjiapkan liang penghabisan
Jang akan terima pusaka: kedamaian antara runtuhan menara
Sudah dulu lagi, sudah dulu lagi
Djari tidak bakal terandjak dari petikan bedil.

LIKE THIS (title supplied)

It's been like this for a long time
The finger doesn't think about pulling the trigger
Don't ask why a finger should be looking for a place like this
I don't know when or why anymore
And don't ask who'll dig the last grave
Whoever inherits the earth: peace in the rubble of a mosque
It's been a long time, a long time
The finger doesn't think about pulling the trigger.

1948

INA MIA

Terbaring dirangkuman pagi
—hari baru djadi—
Ina Mia mentjari
hati impi,
Teraba Ina Mia
kulit harapan belaka
Ina Mia
menarik napas pandjang
ditepi djurang
napsu
jang sudah lepas terhembus,
antara daun-daunan mengelabu
kabut tjinta lama, tjinta hilang
Terasa gentar sedjenak
Ina Mia menekan tapak dihidjau rumput,
Angin ikut
—dajang penghabisan jang mengipas—
Berpaling
kelihatan seorang serdadu mempertjepat langkah ditekongan.

INA MIA

Lying in the lap of morning
—It's just turned light—
Ina Mia tries to find
The heart of her dream.
Ina Mia touches, groping,
Only the rind of hope
Ina Mia
Takes a long breath
Along the edge of the valley
Of passion
That's been blown away.
Among the leaves gone gray as dust
The mist of an old love, a lost love
Is felt trembling for a moment.
Ina Mia stands on the green grass
A breeze springs up
—The last of the fan-waving girls—
She turns away
There's a soldier hurrying around the corner.

1948

PERDJURIT DJAGA MALAM

pro Bahar + Rivai

Waktu djalan. Aku tidak tahu apa nasib waktu?
Pemuda-pemuda jang lintjah jang tua-tua keras, bermata tadjam,
Mimpinja kemerdekaan bintang-bintangnja kepastian
ada disisiku selama mendjaga daerah jang mati ini
Aku suka pada mereka jang berani hidup
Aku suka pada mereka jang masuk menemu malam
Malam jang berwangi mimpi, terlutjut debu . . . . . .
Waktu djalan. Aku tidak tahu apa nasib waktu!

A SENTRY AT NIGHT

for Bahar and Rivai

Time goes on. I don't know where it's going, or why, or when.
Active young men, strong old men, their eyes sharp,
Dreaming of a freedom that's as sure as the stars,
Are at my side as long as you keep watch, here
     in this no-man's land.
I like people who dare to live
I like people who try to discover the night
The night that's fragrant with dreams, rising out of
    the dust . . . . . .
Time goes on. I don't know where it's going. Or why. Or when!

1948

PUNTJAK

Pondering, pondering on you, dear . . . . . .

Minggu pagi disini. Kederasan ramai kota jang terbawa
tambah penjoal dalam diri—diputar atau memutar—
terasa tertekan; kita berbaring bulat telandjang
Sehabis apa terutjap dikelam tadi, kita habis kata sekarang.
Berada 2000 m. djauh dari muka laut, silang siur pelabuhan,
djadi terserah pada perbandingan dengan
tjemara bersih hidjau, kali jang bersih hidjau

Maka tjintaku sajang, kutjoba mendjabat tanganmu
mendekap wadjahmu jang asing, meraih bibirmu dibalik rupa.
Kau terlompat dari randjang, lari ketingkap jang
masih mengandung kabut, dan kau lihat disana, bahwa antara
tjemara bersih hidjau dan kali gunung bersih hidjau
mengembang djuga tanja dulu, tanja lama, tanja.

138

ON TOP OF THE MOUNTAIN

Pondering, pondering on you, dear . . . . . .

It's Sunday morning, here. The excitement of the pushing,
    crowded city, heaping problems
Onto problems—whether spinning or spun—
Feels quieter, calmer; we're lying in bed, naked.
After what we said before, in the darkness, we're out of words,
    now.
Because we're 6,000 feet away from the sea, from the crossing and
    criss-crossing of the harbor,
That world down there seems to be nothing at all compared to
The bright green fir trees, the bright green river.

So, my love, my darling, I try to cling to your hand
To hug your unknown face, to find your reluctant lips.
You jump out of bed, run to the tiny window still
Stuffed with fog, and there you see, between
The bright green fir trees and the bright green mountain stream
The old question still growing, blooming, the old, old question,
    the question.

1948

* *In English in the original*

BUAT GADIS RASID

Antara
daun-daun hidjau
padang lapang dan terang
anak-anak ketjil tidak bersalah, baru bisa lari-larian
burung-burung merdu
hudjan segar dan menjebur
bangsa muda mendjadi, baru bisa bilang "aku"
Dan
angin tadjam kering, tanah semata gersang
pasir bangkit mentanduskan, daerah dikosongi
Kita terapit, tjintaku
—mengetjil diri, kadang bisa mengisar setapak—
Mari kita lepas, kita lepas djiwa mentjari djadi merpati
Terbang
mengenali gurun, sonder ketemu, sonder mendarat
—the only possible non-stop flight
Tidak mendapat.

FOR MISS GADIS RASID

Among
The green leaves
The bright, wide fields
The tiny, innocent children, just old enough to run
The sweetly singing birds
The fresh, fertile rain
The whole new nation, just old enough to say "Me"
And
The sharp, dry wind, the barren soil
The swirling, eroding sand, areas stripped of everything
We are squeezed in, my love
—Compressed, condensed, sometimes able to take
    a single step—
Let's run off, free our searching souls to be like doves
Let's fly
Learn the ways of the desert, not ever meeting, not ever touching
    the ground
—*The only possible non-stop flight* *
In vain.

1948

* *In English in the original.*

Selama bulan menjinari dadanja djadi pualam
randjang padang putih tiada batas
sepilah panggil-panggilan
antara aku dan mereka jang bertolak
Aku bukan lagi sitjilik tidak tahu djalan
dihadapan berpuluh lorong dan gang
menimbang:
ini tempat terikat pada Ida dan ini ruangan "pas bebas"
Selama bulan menjinari dadanja djadi pualam
randjang padang putih tiada batas
sepilah panggil-panggilan
antara aku dan mereka jang bertolak
Djuga ibuku jang berdjandji
tidak meninggalkan sekotji.

Lihatlah tjinta djingga luntur:
Dan aku jang pilih
tindjauan mengabur, daun-daun sekitar gugur
rumah tersembunji dalam tjemara rindang tinggi
pada djendela katja tiada bajang datang mengambang
Gundu, gasing, kuda-kudaan, kapal-kapalan didjaman kanak,
Lihatlah tjinta djingga luntur:
Kalau datang nanti topan adjaib
menggulingkan gundu, memutarkan gasing
mematju kuda-kudaan, menghembus kapal-kapalan
aku sudah lebih dulu kaku

WHILE THE MOON GLEAMS (title supplied)

While the moon gleams on marbled breasts
Stretched out in that endless white field
The greetings that pass from me to those who have departed
Will be terribly quiet.
I'm no longer a child who doesn't know the way
Through alleys and passageways.
I consider:
This place ties me to Ida, and that room's a "passport to freedom.'
While the moon gleams on marbled breasts
Stretched out in that endless white field
The greetings that pass from me to those who have departed
Will be terribly quiet.
And my mother, too, who promised
Not to abandon ship.

See the yellow-gold love fade:
And for me who have chosen
The image blurs, the leaves around are falling
The house disappears into tall leafy fir trees
No shadows float across the window pane.
The marbles. The top. The hobby-horse. The toy boats.
See the yellow-gold love fade:
When the strange storm strikes,
Rolling the marbles, spinning the top,
Spurring on the hobby-horse, blowing the little boats
I'll be long since stiffened.

1948

AKU BERKISAR ANTARA MEREKA

Aku berkisar antara mereka sedjak terpaksa
Bertukar rupa dipinggir djalan, aku pakai mata mereka
pergi ikut mengundjungi gelanggang bersenda:
kenjataan-kenjataan jang didapatnja
(bioskop Capitol putar film Amerika
lagu-lagu baru irama mereka berdansa)
Kami pulang tidak kena apa-apa
Sungguhpun adjal matjam rupa djadi tetangga
Terkumpul dihalte, kami tunggu trem dari kota
Jang bergerak dimalam hari sebagai gigi masa
Kami, timpang dan pintjang, negatip dalam djandi djuga
Sandarkan tulang belulang pada lampu djalan sadja
Sedang tahun gempita terus berkata
Hudjan menimpa. Kami tunggu trem dari kota
Ah hati kami dalam malam ada doa
Bagi jang batja tulisan tanganku dalam tjinta mereka
Semoga segala sypilis dan segala kusta
(Sedikit lagi bertambah derita bom atom pula)
Ini buktikan tanda kedaulatan kami bersama
Terimalah duniaku antara jang menjaksikan bisa
Kualami kelam dan mereka dalam hatiku pula

I RUN AROUND WITH THEM

I run around with them, what else can I do, now—
Changing my face at the edge of the street, I use their eyes
And tag along to visit the fun-house:
These are the facts as I know them
(A new American flick at the Capitol,
The new songs they dance to).
We go home: there's nothing doing
Though this kind of Death is our neighbor, our friend, now.
Hanging around at the corner, we wait for the city bus
That glows night to day like a gold tooth;
Lame, deformed, negative, we
Lean our boney asses against lamp poles
And jaw away the years.
It's raining. We wait for the city bus.
And ah my heart, in this darkness we are a prayer
That whoever reads what this hand writes, writes out of love
        for them,
Will be all those rotting with syphilis, with leprosy
(Add at least those charred by atomic bombs).
This proving our divine rightness
My world will suddenly be O.K., to those who can bear witness—
Darkness, and them: both are in my heart, both.

1949

BUAT NJONJA N.

Sudah terlampau puntjuk pada tahun jang lalu,
dan kini dia turun kerendahan datar.
Tiba dipuntjak dan dia sungguh tidak tahu,
Burung-burung asing bermain keliling kepalanja
dan buah-buah hutan gandjil mentjap warna pada gaun.

Sepandjang djalan dia terkenang akan djadi satu
atas puntjak tinggi sendiri
berdjubah angin, dunia dibawah dan lebih dekat kematian.
Tapi hawa tinggal hampa, tiba dipuntjak dia sungguh tidak tahu
Djalan jang dulu tidak akan dia tempuh lagi,
Selandjutnja tidak ada burung-burung asing, buah-buah pandan
        gandjil
Turun terus. Sepi.
Datar-lebar tidak bertepi.

FOR MRS N.

That was too high a mountain, last year,
So she's climbing down where it's flat.
She got to the peak and didn't know it,
Strange birds were flitting around her head
And queer bits of forest rubbed their colors on her coat.

Along the way she remembers there was someone
All alone, up on the peak,
Wrapped in the wind and the world, and knowing more
    about death.
But the air stayed empty, she got to the top and didn't know it,
She won't risk that first road again,
From now on there'll be no strange birds, no odd patches of
    fragrant pine.
She's going right down. Lonely.
The great flat plain has no edges.

1949

MIRAT MUDA, CHAIRIL MUDA

Dipegunungan 1943.

Dialah, Miratlah, ketika mereka rebah,
menatap lama kedalam pandangnja
tjoba memisah matanja menantang
jang satu tadjam dan djudjur jang sebelah.

Ketawa diadukannja giginja pada
mulut Chairil; dan bertanja: "Adakah, adakah
kau selalu mesra dan aku bagimu indah?"
Mirat raba urut Chairil, raba dada
Dan tahulah dia kini, bisa katakan
dan tundjukkan degan pasti dimana
menghidup djiwa, menghembus njawa
Liang djiwa-njawa saling berganti. Dia rapatkan

Dirinja pada Chairil makin sehati;
hilang setjepuh segan, hilang setjepuh tjemas
Hiduplah Mirat dan Chairil dengan deras,
menuntut tinggi tidak setapak berdjarak dengan mati.

MIRAT'S YOUNG, CHAIRIL'S YOUNG

In the mountains, 1943.

Here you are, Mirat, now they're lying still,
He's staring quietly at that look of yours,
Trying to tell the difference between
One defiant eye and the simple one alongside it.

She rubs her teeth on
Chairil's lips, and asks: "Will you always
Always love me, find me beautiful forever?"
Mirat caresses Chairil, strokes his chest
And now she knows, she can explain it
And she can point to just precisely where
The soul is located, where the center of life breathes.
Soul and life, life and soul, take turns in that passageway. She's
      close, closer,

She and Chairil join, are one;
No more modesty, no more worrying.
Mirat and Chairil live fast, very fast,
Trying as hard as they can not to be separated in this death.

1949

JANG TERAMPAS DAN JANG LUPUT

Kelam dan angin lalu mempesiang diriku,
menggigir djuga ruang dimana dia jang kuingin,
malam tambah merusak, rimba djadi semati tugu.

di Karet, di Karet (daerahku j.a.d.) sampai djuga deru angin

aku berbenah dalam kamar, dalam diriku djika kau datang
dan aku bisa lagi lepaskan kisah baru padamu;
tapi hanja tangan jang bergerak lantang.

tubuhku diam dan sendiri, tjerita dan peristiwa berlaku beku.

150

SOME ARE PLUNDERED, SOME ESCAPE

Darkness and a passing wind purify me.
I shiver, and so does the great room where the one I want is lying.
Night squeezes down, jungle trees freeze like columns of stone.

At Karet, at Karet (where I go next), the cold wind moans too.

I'm tidying my room, and my heart, in case you come
And I can set free a new story for you.
But now it's only my hands that move fiercely.

My body is still, alone. The story, whatever can happen:
     all stiff, icy.

1949

DERAI-DERAI TJEMARA

tjemara menderai sampai djauh,
terasa hari akan djadi malam,
ada berapa dahan ditingkap merapuh,
dipukul angin jang terpendam.

aku sekarang orangnja bisa tahan,
sudah berapa waktu bukan kanak lagi,
tapi dulu memang ada suatu bahan,
jang bukan dasar perhitungan kini.

hidup hanja menunda kekalahan,
tambah terasing dari tjinta sekolah rendah,
dan tahu, ada jang tetap tidak diutjapkan,
sebelum pada achirnja kita menjerah.

FIR TREES IN ROWS

Fir trees straggle into the distance.
I feel day becoming night,
There are branches poking at the tiny window,
Pushed by some unseen wind.

I can stand it, now,
It's been a long time since I was a child.
But once, once there was something
That, now, counts for nothing at all.

Life only puts off defeat,
Extending further and further from simple puppy love
As we learn there's always something unsaid
Before, finally, we give it all up.

1949

Biar malam kini lalu,
tjinta, tapi mimpi masih ganggu
jang bawa kita bersama sekamar
tinggi seperti gua dan sebisu
stasion achir jang dingin
dimalam itu banjak berdjedjer siur katil-katil
Kita terbaring dalam sebuah
jang paling djauh terpentjil.

Bisikan kita tidak patju waktu
kita bertjiuman, aku gembira
atas segala tingkahmu,
sungguhpun jang lain disisiku
dengan mata berisi dendam
dan tangan lesu djatuh
melihat dari randjang.

Apakah dosa, apakah salah
ketjemasan berlimpah sesal
jang djadikan aku korban
kau lantas lakukan dengan tidak sangsi
apa jang tidak bakal aku setudju?
dengan lembut kau tjeritakan
kau sudah terima orang lain
dan penuh sedih merasa
aku orang ketiga dan lantas djalan

LET THIS EVENING GO BY (title supplied)

Let this evening go by, now,
My love—yet the dream still chafes, the dream
That brought us together here in this room
High as a cave and mute,
The last cold station
In that night lined with criss-crossed beds.
We lie on the one
Set furthest apart.

Our whispers don't push at time.
We kiss, I'm delighted
With everything you do,
Even though the others alongside me
Are watching from their beds
With hate in their eyes
And slack, exhausted hands.

Where's the sin, why the blame,
The uneasiness flooded with regret
That turns me sacrificial
When quickly, not hesitating, you manage
What I'd never meant to agree to?
Softly you tell me
You've taken someone else
And, full of sadness, feeling
The odd man out, I quickly leave.

1949

Aku berada kembali. Banjak jang asing:
air mengalir tukar warna, kapal-kapal, elang-elang
serta mega jang tersandar pada chatulistiwa lain;

rasa laut telah berubah dan kupunja wadjah
djuga disinari matari
lain.

Hanja
Kelengangan tinggal tetap sadja.
Lebih lengang aku dikelak-kelok djalan;
lebih lengang pula ketika berada antara
jang mengharap dan jang melepas.

Telinga kiri masih terpaling
ditarik gelisah jang sebentar-sebentar seterang guruh.

I'M BACK AGAIN (title supplied)

I'm back again. There's a lot that's strange:
The flowing water has changed color, the ships, the eagles,
Also the clouds held up, now, by a different equator.

The taste of the sea has changed and my face
Too is lit by a sun
That's different.

Only
The loneliness remains unchanged.
I'm lonelier when the road winds,
Lonelier still when I'm between
Those who hope and those who let go.

My left ear is still bent to the side
Drawn by anxiety sometimes as bright as thunder.

1949

Mari
Kita kosongkan daerah ini
menurut rantjangan jang dari dulu
sudah tertentu

dan satu-satu
isi tempat jang paling termadju

Sebelum bertolak
kita gunduli pohon-pohon jang melambai
kita tjukuri perempuan jang berambut melambai

rindu djangan meretak

LET'S LEAVE HERE (title supplied)

Let's
Leave here
Just as we planned, just
As we agreed
Once

And one by one
Give up everything
In this most progressive of worlds

Before we go
Let's strip the waving trees
Let's shave off women's long, waving hair

But don't lay a hand on desire

(unrevised fragment, 1949?)

Prose[*]

[*] In the text of these translations a double ellipsis (. . . . .) shows a stylistic device common in Indonesian writing, a kind of long, indeterminate pause. The ellipsis (. . .), showing an editorial deletion, occurs only in "Radio Talk, 1946," toward the end, in one case eliminating a reference to the printed source for a poem about to be read, in the second case eliminating the texts of six poems by other Indonesian poets.

THREE AGAINST FATE (*TIGA MENGUAK TAKDIR*), 1950.

CHAIRIL ANWAR, RIVAI APIN, ASRUL SANI

Preface (Pendahuluan)

Three Against Fate was conceived by the three of us—Chairil, Rivai, Asrul—a year and a half ago. The idea came to us when we were planning to start *The Arena (Gelanggang)*. We then thought we would make *The Arena* into a gathering place for the arts (*Kunstkring*). But afterwards we saw that simply bringing things together still would not create, as we had at first thought, a spiritual foundation that could account for the destiny of those who would come together (and appear in) this gathering place. We felt most strongly that what was needed was not simply a new coming together, but a whole new generation. And not only was this necessary; it was also necessary that the new generation have its own life-philosophy, its own sense of destiny.

In discussing our generation's philosophical difficulties we three found ourselves thinking and feeling alike. Our affinity does not mean adherence to one uniform line, nor to a line laid down by any one of us: we value each other because of what we each of us confront. A single fundamental line, we say, isn't even worth arguing about. It was then that we decided to publish this book; the poems in it speak for themselves.

Epigraph

In memory of a beginning that will never end.

AN UNTITLED SPEECH: 1943 (*PIDATO, 1943*)

[Delivered 7 July 1943, before the Japanese-sponsored Youth Organization's Cultural Center (*Angkatan Baru Pusat Kebudajaan*).]

MOTTO:

We wobble along,
One whack and down we go,

All day long we hide
Our moaning and groaning

Why not stand straight, shove back,
Snarl:
Tonight the moon will break through the clouds

I didn't want to write this talk like a formal speech, because speeches ruin good conversation.

I've tried to work out a different form. I thought of just clarifying a few things and making some suggestions and now and then saying what I hope will happen.

But that won't satisfy anyone! Ah: why do I talk about "satisfying"? Does *meaning* have so much influence on what we do, what we write? Is that what I'm driving at? Perhaps it's . . . . . . Of course! That's it, that's it exactly! But all I want to ask is this: let each word I say be considered, weighed, approached, calmly, always calmly.

Enough words: here is part of my soul, of me . . . . . . some pages from my diary . . . . . .

At Home, Evening

Ida, Ida, my love.

This time I've quarreled with my Ida! She said I create too little. No! Don't think I'm just defending my own ideas: only one idea, one opinion. About creating by yourself.

From the way she spoke, from the words she used yesterday, it seemed to me that Ida was too much influenced by her unripe friends, young as they are in both body and spirit. I call them "inspirationalists." Like S[am Amir] and A[zhar]. Sometimes, when there are enough of us around, the talk winds its way onto the subject of art, and they say: Pushing at creation gets you there,

164

just all of a sudden! What a discovery! An inspiration! It's true as far as it goes. And I agree with them. But they go further. According to them, we've got to hold onto faith and belief in these times, we've got to go on putting things onto paper. Prose or poetry, it doesn't matter. And . . . . . . that's it, done! But my Ida won't swallow this. Think about it for yourself!

According to them the ideas, the principles of art or of philosophy drop down to us out of the sky, like sunlight, warming us up and ripening just like that! What do you get, that way? Warm chicken shit!! And isn't this what always comes, too, Ida, from your moaning and groaning? Till now our art has been thin, superficial. No more of the old farts. No more gentle breezes of *that* kind!

I'm an artist, Ida. I have to deal sharply, boldly in considering things—and in discarding them.

Listen!

When Beethoven died, they found books full of notes.

The preparatory work for those clear, sweet melodies was marvellously thorough.

His fifth and ninth symphonies didn't just *happen,* my Ida. This great musician prepared himself for years, and only then did a single ripe fruit—ripe on the inside and the outside—get plucked. His *Missa Solemnis* was the work of more than five solid years.

Ida: you've listened to Mozart, I know you have. Simple, beautiful music. But he needed time, too, before he could call himself ready to create. These true artists received everything from God's own hands . . . . . . !!!

Ida! Look, my darling!

Inspiration and inspiration aren't the same thing. Every time your soul trembles, that isn't real inspiration.

165

We have to think, balance, choose, analyze, criticize, and some-times just throw it all out. Then we can tie things together.

If our work is only half-baked, maybe we'll turn into improvisers in the end. Oh, really big improvisers!

But improvised art is nothing compared to art produced by cre-ative power, by thought, by concentration.

This is a question of life and death itself!! Don't Ida, don't close your lovely eyes—a pool of clear glass in which I drown—don't suspect that I'm exaggerating. Believe me, my love, there's noth-ing truer than what I've been saying . . . . . .

One more thing you may not have understood, Ida. Something I don't explain in order to keep our work from having its own stages, its own internal phases. No. Here's my idea: evil and ugliness, moderation, beauty—they all *exist.* We can't ever change that by our writing.

So it's up to us. Only as *real* artists can we give our utmost, every-thing, as nearly as possible!!!

When we read foreign literature, when we listen quietly to Beetho-ven, we'll feel in them an awareness, an excitement of both body and soul—until the two become one.

So I say: thought, ideas count for a great deal in the best works of art; thinking—that is, balancing, weighing, and discarding with careful good sense . . . . . .

Ida, queen of my heart, don't be like the court dancing girls, recit-ing old pantuns while they whirl around, their heads thrown back —ah, what I am saying, do I want to defile the idea of inspira-tion?!!!—just see what figures they have, the women who oppose dancing . . . . . . ! ! !

166

At Home, Evening

Ida! Ida! Ida!

I just thought for a moment of the darling who, to my mind, stands for the new style, the new line for our literature. When we were mounting our bicycles, I whispered to her about the delights of struggling together, the two of us joined in the struggle for art and for our country. Just in passing. But Ida . . . . . damn! Happiness is all of a piece!!!—Right away she was all ears. She squeezed my arm, her eyes gleamed. And her questions showered down on me: I was the one who was scared . . . . . .

She wanted to know everything I felt, everything. Even though she already knew—oh, incense of my faith, my trust—I was no dilettante, not just casually interested in art.

She wanted to know everything all at once; she wouldn't stop asking questions. Until finally I couldn't say a thing. Maybe shyness made me indefinite. I don't know; certainty isn't my way. But freedom is also the rough, vulgar dance of the womb, the smearing, muddying of conception. The young would-be writer must first be a careful inspector, a scratching, probing critic down to the very essence. Everything, everything as far as the hand and the probing, insistent, shining dissecting-knife can go. Everything! Including the sacred banyan trees, till now unapproachable.

But the future writer—real writer!—must climb on, must chop off all the leafy, superfluous branches . . . . . .

An immense, roaring voice whistles and shouts in his ear: Stop! Stop! Hey, Destroyer, Peace-Breaker!

But I've got guts enough to barge right into the house of holiness, right into the parlor itself! I'm not stopping outside in the yard.

I'm going straight on, Ida, straight on, understand?!!!

Sure, resistance gets stronger and stronger. For a while it isn't clear, but true courage takes a firm grip and jumps right through the window of doubt!

Come again!

They think I want: what? A gleaming, dazzling cut diamond that makes you blink to look at it.

And—not just so I can run off, not so I can get away with anything, but so Ida can get to know me better—I want to say that a man can't afford to be confused, disordered. I'm a critic, not a priest or a religious leader. And they have to be critics too.

The trouble is, Ida, that they're too much missionaries, too little critics.

Ah! This pioneering road is a risky one, Ida. But only to keep your-self on it, I know that for sure! And so we're back at that! Will my darling ever hear me: the pillar, the foundation of existence is . . . . . . danger?!!

At Home, Evening

My dear:

From one thing to the next, darling, step by step.

If what came before was a party, now we come to the best part!

But one page of a diary won't complete your dowry. Understand me, Ida! My stuttering progress—I'll soon think about pulling that around right, to give my darling a sense of utter certainty. Do you suppose, my Ida, there's anything reflected in my shining eyes as I write these lines? Do you?

[Japanese] Colonel Jamasaki, Ida! A brave warrior from Attu! Ah, be in harmony with this noble spirit. The personification of the ideal! Observe, my darling, the service given to his Homeland, more and more fervently, by J.M.M. Tenno Heika, the sentiments reaching higher and higher—and I think most of them must be included in that life energy which flares up fantastically, until it is concluded in death. Ida! Vitalism.

Vitality! The fire of life!

We still haven't discussed *beauty.* To me, Ida, beauty is a balancing, a synthesizing of life's vibrations. This is certainly a shorthand explanation; I admit it. But *vitality* is different. There's no sameness about beauty. Vitality is all of a piece, from top to bottom. It's one thing that can't be dragged into creating beauty. In art vitalism is a *chaotisch voorstadium,* a chaotic first phase, while beauty is a *kosmisch eindstadium,* a cosmic final phase.

But, darling, the artist must be a pioneer. He must be courageous, he must be vital. He can't hesitate to plunge into a jungle full of wild animals, to wade into a sea so wide that the other shore is invisible. The artist is a symbol of independence, of the free life.

Don't cut yourself off from existence, isolated, alone!

No, no, forever no! That way you may come to die alone, with no one to bury you. Will and desire are the only core possible for the free life.

We're children of a different age, Ida. Once upon a time they weren't brave enough to be blunt; they always chose devious paths. They even covered themselves with declarations about their views, always talking more and more broadly and generally. But I smell a rat . . . . . . !! We know more, today; our techniques are better. It's only right that we leave them behind; in fact, they already *are* behind, and several long leaps behind. We don't want to take just ordinary pictures, but X-rays right down to the white of the bones. In other words, no one's going to make us play at being life's musical instruments, not any more they're not. We play life's own songs, so we have to be honest, blunt. Because we've got courage and awareness and confidence and the skill too.

We know where we're going, Ida. We're living, now, at a thousand miles an hour! To be definite, to be brief, is not to be empty, no! In a little sentence like "Once it was significant, but it's dead," we can weave all the goals of our life. So you can say we're definite; you can't say we're empty. Don't forget me, don't, Ida. How could you? I know your heart has played at hide-and-seek! Your feelings are meant for the writer of the future, too, though he may have enough feelings of his own! Not feelings that are isolated or simply *there,* but feeling for and in life! Welcome life! Listen to one of my poems, glowing with youthful feeling. Be refreshed!

(Here Anwar transcribes "Invitation" *[Adjakan]* see p. 13)

Thus feeling for life, glowing like the sun, laughing with pleasure, because we're full of the glow of our work . . . . . .

Help me, Ida . . . . . .

LOOKING IT IN THE EYE (*BERHADAPAN MATA*)

[The anonymous "M." was in fact H. B. Jassin, to whom this letter was sent on 25 August 1943, the opening gun in a correspondence abruptly terminated by the Japanese censors. Anwar's letter was published 28 August 1943, Jassin's reply appeared on 4 September 1943—and that was all the occupation authorities allowed.

Beginning with paragraph #12 ("They're horribly influenced by . . .") this essay/letter is a careful reworking of the diary entry already reworked as part of Anwar's 7 July 1943, speech, p. 163.]

Dear M.,

This is my position, as far as I can explain it. And this letter will enable you to guess in what direction my thoughts are running. Like a writer who's just produced a number of small poems and wants to go on—around and around in his own circle—our discussion will automatically deal with particular literary works. Later on we can expand our focus. I'll speak frankly about the plastic arts and music.

But note my first sentence, which in truth I couldn't omit. Further, this whole letter revolves around that sentence.

This is what I mean: my inner and outer "position," my "position" physically and intellectually. Everything of which I'm aware, everything I guess at. What comes close to me, what is me.

If I say that this letter is in reply to your invitation (now six months old) for me to really plunge into the world of Art, it would be assumed that I was neutral on the question—an urgent "question" like that. You'll feel that, and how will it affect you? You've indicated that I ought to play the Art game, though you know almost nothing about me. Or—have I some special sign?!

If I had done what you said from the first, of course I'd just be following along where you led. This has never been my idea; on the contrary, in Art it's impossible. Before you follow along, you need the kind of self-awareness that amounts to a joyous radiation of will and energy. And without that, don't follow anyone! Especially not in Art! Which isn't just a hobby, a passing fancy.

While I've been silent—not sending you any letters—my work has begun to be known—often I push it myself, so help me!— among artists of all points of view here. And it's being read closely, scrutinized with the care given to works of art.

Suddenly I'm making an impression; this is certainly a beginning, some motion, at least a ripple on the quiet waters.

But—I was sure of it before, but it isn't anything, just a wave as big as a house!—but there is a but . . . . . .

Often, in going about with artists I know, I'm startled. Dumbfounded! Because suddenly I find some of them not at all what I imagined (and hoped), with very different ways, talking differently

171

—they prove that they're really clerks, *clerks,* sometimes expert businessmen!

And it's not just I who say this. After studying what these people have produced . . . . . . what a crime, they're all neither this nor that, and slapdash to boot. Aren't they fed up with this sort of thing? If not, when, when . . . . . . ?! I've felt like getting drunk . . . . . . !!!

They're horribly influenced by—let me give it a name—"the law of inspiration." I'll mention two whom I know personally: S[am Amir] and A[zhar]. Pushing at creation suddenly gets you there, just all of a sudden, they say. A real discovery! An inspiration.

But they go further: we must hold onto faith and belief in these times, we must go on putting things onto paper. And . . . . . . that's it, done! But I won't swallow this! If they're right, the ideas, the principles of art or philosophy drop down to us out of the sky, like sunlight, warming us up and ripening just like that! And the result? Of course, neither this nor that! And isn't that just what always comes from moaning and groaning. Till now our art has been thin, superficial. No more of the old windbags. No more gentle gas of *that* sort! Much less their oozing . . . . . . !! The artist, M., must deal sharply, boldly in considering things—and in discarding them. And someone who just follows along won't be able to do this. Because he has no principles of his own; he's still a long way from knowing what he's about. He's powerless.

Listen!

When Beethoven died, they found books full of notes. The preparatory work for those clear, sweet melodies was marvellously thorough. This great musician prepared himself for years, and only then did a single ripe fruit—ripe on the inside and the outside—get plucked. His *Missa Solemnis* was the work of more than five solid years.

Your fiancée, Nur, has surely played Mozart. Simple, beautiful music. But Mozart needed time, too, before he could call himself ready to create. This true artist received everything from God's own hands . . . . . .

We have to think, balance, choose, analyze, criticize, and sometimes just throw it all out. To tie things together!

If our work is neither this nor that, only half-baked, maybe we'll turn into improvisers in the end. Oh, really big improvisers! But improvised art is nothing compared to art produced by creative power, by thought, by concentration. To me this is life and death itself!

Don't, don't think I'm exaggerating! You know that's not my way.

This is how my ideas are running: If our confidence is firmly rooted in the creation of art, all our life will be centered on that alone!

One more thing, M.! What I've set out here is not a "recipe" to keep our writing from having its own stages, its own internal phases. No. Here is its purpose: evil and ugliness, moderation, beauty— they all *exist*. We can't ever change that by our writing. So it's up to us. Only as *real* artists can we give our utmost, everything, as nearly as possible!

When we read foreign writing, when we listen quietly to Beethoven, we'll feel in them an awareness, an excitement of both body and soul, slanted neither to the left nor to the right. It's like this, M.! Thought, ideas, count for a great deal in the best works of art. Thinking: that is, balancing, weighing, and discarding with careful good sense.

Again! I reject simply following along—I'm fed up with timid middle-of-the-roadism. I can't work that way.

Nor am I like court dancing girls, reciting old pantuns while they whirl around, their heads thrown back—ah, but I don't want to defile the idea of inspiration; what am I saying?—just see what

figures they have, the women who oppose dancing . . . . . . !!!
Enough, my friend: my regards to Nur.

HOPPLA! (*HOPPLA!*)

[Published in December, 1945]

Since a man can only write according to beliefs long and deeply held,
don't try to follow a faith that still belongs to the future.

Looking back, we see that *Pudjangga Baru* [*The New Writer*] was created in 1933, at the same time as Hitler's seizure of power in Germany; yet in all its years of publication the magazine printed only a single superficial article on fascism! Set this against the desert of its early issues, the essays without any particular literary skill (in the broadest sense!), all making a great deal of noise about "modernization." Since there was, of course, a certain intensity in the stirring about, the upheavals that were ultimately responsible for *Pudjangga Baru*'s coming into being, it spawned a number of poetry collections. There was Armijn Pané's "The Spirit of Life" (*Djiwa Berdjiwa*): not one poem of this group sticks in the memory. "Scattered Clouds" (*Tebaran Mega*) by Takdir Alisjahbana: two or three poems of mourning, written after his wife's death, are still poignant. Several poems by Or. Mandank have simple, natural lines. The summit of the *Pudjangga Baru* movement's nine years was Amir Hamzah, who contributed lyrical prose, free verse, two collections of poetry, "Fruits of Longing" (*Buah Rindu*) and "Songs of Loneliness" (*Njanji Sunji*), as well as translations from several well-known Oriental literatures, collected in "Incense from the East" (*Setanggi Timur*). Those who knew him well say that Amir Hamzah was influenced by Sufi and Parsi writers. But what seems to me more important to notice is that in "Songs of Loneliness" Amir's clean, pure manner produces poems that, in addition to liberating the poet, also introduce a new style into Indonesian sentences, compactly violent, sharp and yet short. Before Amir one could call the old poetry a destructive force; but what a bright light he shone on the new language. "Songs of Loneliness" can be termed "obscure poetry," *duistere poezie*. That is, we can't understand Amir Hamzah if we read "Songs of Loneliness" without knowing something of history and of religion (Islam), because he uses language that draws on them for illustrations and comparisons. His friend Takdir Alisjahbana places Amir Hamzah in an "international" category; I can agree only to the extent that Amir's poetry is classifiable with the work of certain other contemporary writers. Amir too needs to be read with prior knowledge, the reader also is required to work.

After *Pudjangga Baru* there is a series of other men—Karim Halim, who wrote four or five poetic reminiscences, and Asmara Hadi, who produced some clear battle cries, and some Sepoy love songs. In addition, several critical and polemical pieces without any particular skill or individuality (personality) attempted to put some life into *Pudjangga Baru,* but in truth they contribute nothing to the advancement of literature. Thus, in all its nine years *Pudjangga Baru* was utterly bland; none of the writers I've mentioned achieved real "weight."

Then comes the Japanese "Culture Board," labelled "Cultural Center," which made possible the development of a strictly Greater Asian "art"—castor oil—cotton—increasing farm yields—Indonesians driven to Japan as coolies—put your pennies in the piggy bank—ship-building and all the rest. And also young artists turned into disciplined shock troops, within the confines of Greater Asia-ness, often powerfully confined within those limits!!! They were not allowed to know that hundreds of European artists (Germans, Italians), and even Japanese, when confronted with these spiritual (and physical) risks, left the countries they loved precisely because of such compulsions. Some thought it better not to write than to do violence to truth and progress.

And now: Hoppla! A jump great enough to fulfill the promise of this young nation of ours. After the rebellion against the Word we forgot that the Word spreads its roots, lives from era to era, stuffed with respect and Dreams and Hope. And with Love and Hate. The Word is Truth!!! Let the Word not be enslaved by *two* bosses; let the Word be our one fundamental Principle!! And the past will only teach us that this pushing urgency we're aware of is simply in ourselves; the price of the spirituality we've destroyed is that we must grope our way back in the best style possible. The world—ourselves most of all—when it loses the fullness of its freedom, enjoys recovering the savor of freedom.

Freedom and Responsibility are the price of humanity, the price of this our Existence. And anyone who won't contribute we're prepared to shove along . . . . . .

Hoppla! Hop-hop! Let the pure flame burn, the undying flame of a brotherhood of nations.

Hoppla! Let us be brothers, carving an alabaster monument in honor of a perfect Indonesia. A perfect world . . . . . .

WRITING POEMS, LOOKING AT PICTURES (*MEMBUAT SADJAK, MELIHAT LUKISAN*)

[First printed in June, 1949.]

Poems are made from words, as paintings are made of paint and canvas or sculpture is made from marble, clay, and the like. But those who are moved by the sight of a painting or a piece of sculpture don't think the quality of the paint or the canvas or the marble an important question, a fundamental matter. It's not the materials used that are important, but only what they are used to achieve.

Most people "divide" artistic accomplishment into *form* and *content*. But one cannot formulate a really clear, definite distinction between form and content, which in art not only go hand in hand but reciprocally fulfill one another. And only the feelings of true artists can be turned into really notable forms and styles—they alone can create what we see or read or hear with emotion, what we enthusiastically praise or damn.

If two artists both portray a certain quarter of a city, it may be that we'll admire one painting and the other will strike us as ugly. The difference won't be in the "subject," because here both subjects are the same. The difference *will* be in the feelings that go along with each artist's view of the city and in the way those feelings are expressed.

And just as any one subject may impress two painters, so also two different kinds of subject may produce the same emotions in one and the same painter. A simple picture of a pair of old shoes may be as "lovely" as a vase full of varicolored flowers. Because what we see isn't simply a pair of old shoes but a pair that has been *felt* as "lovely"—because, too, the artist is able to bring this out with lines and with shapes, because he can compel us to acknowledge what his art has produced.

So what is important is this: *using the expressive methods of his art, the artist must focus his efforts on his own emotions.* The tools and devices with which the poet can express himself are the materials of language, which he uses *intuitively.* By "manipulating" the lofty and the low he can achieve a pattern, an organization, and then he can create variations within the pattern—using rhythm as a unifying element. The melody of words can help establish a poem's form as language becomes now heavy and slow, now light and quick. Further, the poet can choose extraordinary words, weighed and considered with great care, or words that solidify and unify his poetic intent. Syntax can be varied, enabling the poet

177

to work with still subtler effects, to suggest the more complex aspects of the human soul. With rhythm and melody, with syntax and word choice and metaphor, the poet makes his poem—and only if the reader is willing (and able) to follow the particular, special details of what the poet has done can he fully understand and appreciate the poem he reads. To experience a poem's loveliness one does not need to be schooled in one or more of these linguistic "tools"; one does need to be cooperative and to have had some practice at identifying or connecting together the elements which go to make up the poem's particular "subject."

But because a poem's subject isn't what determines its artistic worth does *not* mean that a poet can be equally moved by any and all subjects. On the contrary: it's quite clear that some natural events, and some man-made ones, do not affect us; we don't think them "important." Love, birth, death, loneliness, the sun and the moon, religious faith—these are the subjects that perpetually stir the artist.

RADIO TALK, 1946 (*PIDATO RADIO 1946*)

My listening friends:

Every completed poem is an entire world. A world realized, created all over again by the poet. Creating all over again in a different form (matter) and spirit, a different realm (ideal and visual), and a different environment, the poet takes his raw material from other works of art that strike him as significant, that have spiritual affinities for him, and also draws on the thoughts and discoveries of other men, all of which merge in his own imagination—elements, substances previously created by others, all interconnected within him—the cross-grafting becoming a single, rounded unity (beautiful as well as something that moves and stirs others), entirely new, a new world, a world which belongs only to the poet.

To move forward, to grow, means that the creative process experiences this over and over—the poet's ideas coming and going, pouring out: his ideals, his vision, the feelings and the shifts in his own life, his attitudes, the bases of his thought. Everything, everything that goes into the making of this fundamental, essential way *must* be experienced, endured (in his spirit, his aspirations, his emotions, his thoughts, and his own knowledge of life) by the poet himself—must become a part of him, of his gladness and sadness, *his* possessions, belonging to his spirit. And it must be enlarged by the labor of creation—the labor of shaping and forming, of instituting order and pattern by thought and by feeling, of balancing, of considering—until the thing has a life of its own, its own breath and reality, a life and a shape.

My listening friends:

This is the broad outline I've employed in picking the poems I'll read tonight, works by our younger poets.

I'd be talking too much if I went on here to analyze these poems in detail, every little point. I'll read each poem once, therefore, and then indicate briefly its weaknesses and peculiarities, and how these poems differ from and are able to free themselves from the influence of *Pudjangga Baru* ways—the *Pudjangga Baru* poems having been rounded up in an anthology by Sutan Takdir Alisjahbana himself, the boss, the culture-hero of that now-vanished literary movement.

I'll begin with "Year After Year" (*Tahun Bertahun*) by Sularko, which I quote from [the magazine] *Rebirth* (*Pembangunan*).

YEAR AFTER YEAR

Year after year it melts, comes clearer and clearer,
The boundaries shrink, resistance grows weak;
Foam always bubbles away,
From trees, from flowers, in the sky, on the earth.

My heart, which used to climb mountains, which attacked the air,
Forgets where it's been, struck by disaster;
Misery floods over life,
Your wife, your friends, it's a homespun song.

I choose the city, its ways, its struggles,
And my wounds hurt even more;
I hold my heart in my hand,
For better or worse, for pleasure or pain.

This is a short-winded poem, beginning very well, very smoothly; its imagery catches you and says something new; but when it tries to end, it's pushed, it's forced, and the idea falters, peters out. In form it still follows the *Pudjangga Baru* tradition.

The second poem is a portrait by a young lady named Walujati.

PARTING

Together we braid flowers
Into a delicate, fragrant bouquet,
Returning home, happy,
As the red ball drops down from the sky.

At the side-road we part.
The bouquet trembles in our hands,
Falls, and breaks in two.

I take one half, you the other
And, holding it firmly, you are gone . . . . . .

I walk alone in the dusk,
You run away with only the flower
Sending its scent to me.

"Parting" is a beautiful poem, and a successfully romantic one, in the sense that it succeeds in its imaginative portrait. It too is, in form, in the *Pudjangga Baru* tradition.

180

The poets I'll introduce, from here on, are Sakti Alamsjah, Rivai Apin, and Muhammad Akbar Djuhana. These poets have no connection with *Pudjangga Baru;* they are very much their own men.

I'll read poems by each of them, but I'll save for next week my detailed analysis and explanations. . . .

THREE APPROACHES, ONE IDEA (*TIGA MUKA, SATU POKOK*)

[1947]

1.

Once, during a get-together at S. S. [Sutan Sjahrir?]'s house, a woman friend said that she too lived with the sense of something profound and vast, except that *she could not express it.*

I was sitting beside her, and I asked what she was trying to say:

"Unless I'm wrong, you mean to say that art can be divided into the ability to express ideas and the ability to express emotions. How false! Art is the *conscious creation* of thoughts *and* feelings. You want to think that you've attained that level, but in fact the psychological, the organic resemblances between you and a poet are, to say the least, very obscure."

"I don't have your technical ability [she replied], no, and I don't care to reveal what's in *my* heart."

"All right: let's say that you could *think and feel* as daringly as that 'madman,' Nietzsche. Let's say that you could also have a profound sense of the tragedy of human existence. But don't tell me that when something happens that pleases or pains you, you can simply store it away—that, like Beethoven, you can turn pain and sorrow into utter bliss?"

"Why not [she continued]? I'm not like a poet because I'm not free to reveal my feelings. This might be thought an act of discretion on my part."

"Let's go on: I don't want to get sidetracked into this question of discretion, not yet! If I understand you, you say art is solely rooted in technique. Fine! But how do you explain this phenomenon: two painters with the same precise technical attainments but who despise one another? *Doesn't this mean that such aversions can't be avoided?* And that these aversions are founded on something other than thought and emotion, something else which *impels* them and not the two men's own thoughts and emotions?"

"But . . . . . . ?"

"Let's continue: the greater the technique, you say, the greater the art produced. Let me contradict that with an example. Basuki Abdullah [a painter] has a finer technique than Affandi [a more famous painter], whose work is wonderfully passionate, emotional; if we're still talking about technique, Abdullah paints academic stuff that is the exact opposite of every worthwhile piece of art being created these days. Affandi has the power to move you, but we look at Abdullah's canvases and are unaffected. Affandi *lives* more profoundly and more truthfully; Affandi is mature enough to experience life, because it's with awe that he unfolds his own life; that's why 'an Affandi can only be by Affandi.' Between the two painters there's a difference in intensity, in intention, and in the purpose of experience—there's no contact likely between them, no common meeting ground."

2. My Friend and I (Kawan dan Aku: satu rangka rentjana)
(An Outline)

I give a party in honor of my friend's arrival. Perhaps he's just flown both the Atlantic and the Pacific at the same time, or is returning from the very highest peak in the Himalayas. All the newspapers are fighting to praise him most, to idealize him.

I take his hand, I welcome him, but suddenly he answers, rather rudely: "You too want to bother me? Let the newspapers make their fuss, but when we're alone let's have no more of it! You know, damn it, that the ones who still aren't finished glorifying me are some of the same newspapers that, before, read me out of society, sent me beyond the pale. I can't split myself in two, I can't. I live, I exist as a totality, one single indivisible whole. I have the right to speak the truth about myself. And I've a right, also, to the pleasure I experience in indicating that I *must* speak out."

My friend is silent a moment. Then, his voice fuller, richer, he says: "Everyone else has only enough courage to become a *part* of themselves; they try as hard as they can to keep from being whole people, from being themselves alone. They're all carbon copies. They choose the model they ape by seeing what everyone else is imitating. There aren't many people of a different sort. We're just not brave enough, we haven't the courage. Not brave enough even to be ourselves! This fear of our own moral capacities is the greatest traitor in existence. And we claim to love life. We can achieve it only for ourselves."

He's silent again. Then he speaks once more:

"Not long ago a lot of people asked if I were writing anything, if I'd kept notes of my experiences, my travels. Of course not! I refuse to; I can't whittle away at dead pleasures. On the contrary, it's by forgetting everything that's been that I communicate, that I concentrate on the here and now. I don't believe in anything dead. I never look back; my existence can't be blurred by regret."

I stand there quietly listening to these rough words, trying to think of a response, and then suddenly I find one: "Can't you just ask everybody to be different from everybody else?"

And suddenly my friend—huge, enormous, looking for a moment as if he meant to blow his top!—turns away, says not another word, leaves me, leaves my party.

3. A Proclamation (*Pemberian Tahu*)

> I don't intend to share fate,
> Fate which is a universal loneliness.
> I chose you out of the lot of them, but
> It won't be long before we're tangled in loneliness again.
> Once I really wanted you:
> In the vast night, becoming little children again,
> We kissed and clung and were never bored,
> I felt I could never let you go.
> Don't tie your life to mine,
> I can't be with anyone for long.
> And this, too, I'm writing on board ship, from the sea that has no name!

FOUR APHORISMS

[Found, says H. B. Jassin, who prints them at pages 117, 120, 125, and 131 of his *Chairil Anwar: Pelopor Angkatan '45* (*Chairil Anwar: Pioneer of the Generation of '45*), "on loose sheets in Anwar's notebooks or among notes written on only one or two pages."]

1. Living under the Japanese, we had to act—it was doubly necessary, at least to keep our minds and our senses alert, to counteract the atmosphere that surrounded us, to keep from losing our self-respect.

2. An era of "ism's" is a one-sided party for one-sided dancers. What I admire is the violence, the passion with which they brawl!

3. Message for the younger generation: wisdom and insight aren't enough; you've got to work up energy and enthusiasm.

4. We've got to find our compensations and complexes for ourselves. Compensations and complexes: a huge warehouse, the dark home of our real hidden self.

EXCERPTS FROM LETTERS TO H. B. JASSIN

1. Letter Dated 8 March 1944:

In our circle the habit of fence-sitting is endemic. You know this, of course. I entered art wholeheartedly—but to this moment I've been able to participate in the *externals* of the art world only in a halfhearted way. But luckily what's inside is all desire, and from the time I was fifteen years old I've headed for only one goal: art.

2. Another Letter of the Same Date:

No, I'm not going back to the kind of prose I used in my talk to the "New Generation"! Prose like that really soars, right up to the highest clouds, because in the intensity of writing I feel all whipped up; but looking it over again carefully, I see that with that sort of prose I can't get to an accounting. And what I want is to reach an absolute accounting with everything around me.

And the lines I've arrived at are *human dignity* and *personality.* It's shaky ground, I know that too, and it's the same anywhere, even if I stick to literature, the plastic arts, and drama.

My prose, and my poetry too, have to be scraped and dug, *word by word,* as far down as I can get, down to the center of the word, the core of the image.

3. Letter Dated 10 April 1944:

What I've sent you—what I call poems!—are only attempts at new imagery.

They're not truly finished work! There are still many "stages of trying" for me to go through before I turn out real poems.

Appendixes

Appendix A

NOTES ON THE INDONESIAN ORIGINALS*

Abbreviations:

Deru Tjampur Debu = DTD
Jang Terampas dan Jang Putus = JT
Tiga Menguak Takdir = TMT
H. B. Jassin, *Chairil Anwar, Pelopor Angkatan 45* = Jassin

I have in general preferred Jassin's text, when available. DTD has been given the next most authoritative position; JT next; and TMT last. This is because Jassin is in possession of Chairil Anwar manuscripts, and because he has plainly tried to be as accurate, in all things, as he possibly can be; because DTD, although I do not know who edited it, seems, in general, later and more authoritative than JT (the latter was apparently printed, in large part, from a typescript circulated during the Japanese Occupation); and because TMT contains no poems not elsewhere collected in book form and also because it seems, at times, to have been proofread distinctly more carelessly than the other volumes (see, e.g., "Sadjak Buat Basuki Resobowo").

Variant lines, words, word-order, spellings, and punctuation are indicated by italics. Punctuation and capitalization are in general separately noted as well.

SIA-SIA (p. 10): In DTD and JT
The text in JT, as is often the case in JT, begins each line with a capital letter
line 2, JT: Membawa *kembang berkarang*
line 3, JT: no colon at end of line
line 4, JT: Sutji capitalized
                no period at end of line

---

* *Only textual variants are discussed in these notes. For other matters see Appendix B.*

line 6, JT: *u*ntukmu not capitalized
line 7, JT: *Lalu* kita sama termanggu
line 8, JT: *a*pakah not capitalized
line 9, JT: Tjinta? *Kita berdua* tak mengerti
               no period at end of line
line 10, JT: Sehari kita bersama . . .
               no period at end of line

ADJAKAN (p. 12): In Jassin and JT
line 1, JT: missing
line 5, JT: Petjah pentjar sekarang
line 9, JT: Bersepeda sama gandengan
line 10, JT: followed by stanza space
line 13, JT: Gembira girang
line 15, JT: Kita mandi basahkan diri

AKU (p. 20): In Jassin, DTD, and JT
line 2, JT: *kutahu* tak seorang 'kan meraju
line 4, JT: exclamation point at end of line
line 5, JT: *D*jalang capitalized
line 6, JT: Dari *kumpulan* terbuang
line 10, JT: followed by stanza space
line 11, JT: Hingga hilang pedih *dan* peri
               period at end of line
line 12, Jassin and JT: not followed by stanza space
line 13, JT: period at end of line

PENERIMAAN (p. 30): In Jassin, DTD, and JT
line 1, JT: *Djika* kau mau, kuterima kau kembali
line 3, Jassin: Aku masih   sendiri
line 7, JT: *Djika* kau mau, kuterima kau kembali
line 8, JT: *Tapi untukku sendiri*
line 9, JT: no period at end of line

190

KESABARAN (p. 32): In DTD and JT
line   3, JT: Dunia djauh—mengabur
line   7, JT: Aku hendak *berbitjara*
line   8, JT: Suaraku hilang, tenaga*ku* terbang
line   9, JT: *T*idak capitalized
             colon instead of exclamation point at end of line
line 10, JT: not followed by stanza space
line 11, JT: Keras-membeku air kali
line 12, JT: period at end of line
line 14, JT: sambil not capitalized
             followed by stanza space
line 15, JT: m*u*sti

RUMAHKU (p. 38): In Jassin and JT
line 12, JT: period at end of line

HAMPA (p. 40): In DTD and JT
dedication, DTD: Kepada Sri
line   1, JT: comma after diluar
             sepi not capitalized
             no period at end of line
line   2, JT: Lurus-kaku pohonan   Tak bergerak
line   3, JT: line ends with kepuntjak; Sepi memagut, followed by no punc-
             tuation, is separate following line
line   4, JT: Tak *suatu* kuasa-*berani* melepas *diri*
line   5, JT: Segala menanti. Menanti-*menanti*
line   6, JT: period at end of line
line   7, JT: *Dan* ini menanti *penghabisan* mentjekik
line   8, JT: mentjekung instead of mentjengkung
line   9, JT: omitted
line 10, JT: line ends with bertuba, followed by punctuation; a com-
             pletely different line follows:
             Rontok-gugur segala. Setan bertempik
line 11, JT: Ini sepi terus ada. *Menanti. Menanti*

KAWANKU DAN AKU (p. 42): In DTD and JT
dedication, DTD: omitted
line 1, JT: Kami *djalan sama. Sudah* larut
line 2, JT: period at end of line
line 3, JT: period at end of line
              followed by stanza space
line 4, JT: period at end of line
line 5, JT: mengental-pekat; tumpat-pedat
              period at end of line
line 6, JT: Siapa *berkata?*
              followed by stanza space
line 8, JT: period at end of line
line 9, JT: exclamation point at end of line
line 11, JT: Hingga *hilang* segala makna

KEPADA PEMINTA-MINTA (p. 52): In Jassin, DTD, and JT
line 1, JT: no comma between baik and aku
line 4, DTD: no period at end of line
line 7, JT: Nanah meleleh dari *luka*
line 16, JT: Mengum instead of mengaum
line 17, JT: no comma between baik and aku

SELAMAT TINGGAL (p. 54): In Jassin, DTD, and JT
subtitle: appears on original manuscript, appears in no collected version
line 1, JT: followed by separate line:
                        Bukan buat kepesta
line 4, JT: seru-menderu
line 11, JT: ends with double ellipsis
              followed by stanza space

(kita gujah lemah) (p. 62): in Jassin and JT
line 7, Jassin: *bulan* instead of purnama

SADJAK PUTIH (p. 72): In DTD and TMT
dedication: on original manuscript and in TMT
line   1, TMT: Bersandar pada tari *bewarna* pelangi
line   2, TMT: sut*e*ra
line   4, TMT: period at end of line
line   6, TMT: Meria*h* instead of Meriak
line   8, TMT: *Menari* instead of Menarik
                     period at end of line
line 10, TMT: not followed by stanza space
line 11, TMT: Selama   darah mengalir dari luka

LAGU SIUL (p. 82) Part II: In DTD and JT
line   1 (of Part II), JT: colon at end of line
line   2 (of Part II), JT: no colon at end of line
line   4 (of Part II), JT: period at end of line
line   6 (of Part II), JT: no comma at end of line
line 10 (of Part II), JT: no comma at end of line

ORANG BERDUA (p. 86): In Jassin and DTD
title: on manuscript, "With Mirat," "Dengan Mirat"
line 2, DTD: period at end of line
line 5, DTD: 'kan
line 8, DTD: period at end of line

TJATETAN TH. 1946 (p. 92): In Jassin, DTD, and TMT
title, TMT: Tjat*a*tan Th. 1946
line   4, Jassin: not followed by stanza space
line   8, Jassin: not followed by stanza space
line 10, DTD: semi-colon at end of line
line 11, DTD: . . . diserahkan *ke*pada anak lahir sempat
line 12, TMT: tetap

TJERITA BUAT DIEN TAMAELA (p. 98): In DTD and TMT
line 5, TMT: no period at end of line
line 10, TMT: . . . *pen*djaga hutan pala
                no period at end of line
line 12, TMT: no period at end of line
line 14, TMT: no comma at end of line
line 20, TMT: exclamation point after Awas
line 23, TMT: no comma after dimalam

SENDJA DI PELABUHAN KETJIL (p. 104): In DTD and TMT
line 4, DTD: *dari* instead of diri

TJINTAKU DJAUH DIPULAU (p. 106): In Jassin, DTD, and TMT
line 2, TMT: no period at end of line
line 3, TMT: no comma at end of line
line 4, TMT: no comma at end of line
line 7, TMT: no comma at end of line
line 16, Jassin: no period at end of line

KEPADA KAWAN (p. 114): In Jassin and DTD
line 1, DTD: *Adjal* capitalized
line 3, Jassin: not followed by stanza space
line 8, Jassin: not followed by stanza space
line 11, DTD: no comma at end of line
line 19, Jassin: not followed by stanza space

SADJAK BUAT BASUKI RESOBOWO (p. 118): In Jassin and TMT
title, Jassin: this poem and "Heaven," "Sorga," printed under the general heading: "Two Poems for Basuki Resobowo,"
"Dua Sadjak buat Basuki Resobowo"

line 2, TMT: le*t*ih instead of lebih
line 4, TMT: no comma at end of line
line 8, TMT: baj*i* instead of baju
line 13, TMT: b*a*ku instead of beku

SORGA (p. 120): In Jassin and DTD
line 4, DTD: Muhammadyah instead of Muhammadijah

KRAWANG-BEKASI (p. 126): In Jassin, JT, and TMT
line 2, TMT: no period at end of line
line 6, TMT: not followed by stanza space
line 8, Jassin: no period at end of line
line 17, TMT: forms last part of line 16, instead of a separate line
line 19, TMT: not followed by stanza space
line 31, TMT: *J*ang capitalized
line 32, TMT: *b*erbaring instead of terbaring
line 32, Jassin: no period at end of line

PERDJURIT DJAGA MALAM (p. 136): In JT and TMT
dedication: not in JT
line 1, TMT: no question mark at end of line
line 4, TMT: ada disisiku selama *kau* mendjaga . . .
              period at end of line
              followed by stanza space
line 7, TMT: berwangimimpi as one word instead of two
              *ber*lutjut instead of terlutjut
line 8, TMT: period instead of exclamation point at end of line

AKU BERKISAR ANTARA MEREKA (p. 144): in *Ipphos Report,* Feb. 1949, and in *Horison* (edited by H. B. Jassin), April 1968. I have followed the text in *Horison,* attributing to it the authority here consistently accorded Jassin's texts of Chairil Anwar.

line 1: followed by a period, in *Ipphos*
line 4: followed by a period, in *Ipphos*
line 5: followed by a comma, in *Ipphos*
line 8: *Adjal* capitalized, in *Ipphos;* line ends with period, in *Ipphos;* followed by stanza space, in *Ipphos*
line 10: followed by a period, in *Ipphos*
line 12: followed by a comma, in *Ipphos*
line 13: followed by a period, in *Ipphos*
line 14: followed by a period, in *Ipphos*
line 21: In *Ipphos: Kualami kelam* malam *dan mereka dalam* diriku *pula;* followed by a period, in *Ipphos*

BUAT NJONJA N. (p. 146)
Line 9 reads ". . . *dia* sugguh *tidak tahu*" in *Ipphos Report.* Since this is almost certainly a typographical error for ". . . *dia* sungguh *tidak tahu,*" as in line 3, I have corrected the text as here printed.

JANG TERAMPAS DAN JANG LUPUT (p. 150): in JT and TMT
title: see Notes on the English Versions, p. 202.
line 2, TMT: *Menggigir* capitalized
line 3, TMT: *Malam* capitalized
line 4, TMT: *Di* capitalized
    dingin instead of angin
line 5, TMT: *Aku* capitalized
    *hati*ku instead of diriku
    comma at end of line
line 5, JT: kaudatang as one word instead of two
line 6, TMT: *Dan* capitalized
    comma instead of semi-colon at end of line
line 7, TMT: *Tapi* capitalized
    Tapi *kini* hanja tangan . . .
line 8, TMT: *Tubuhku* capitalized
    berla*lu* instead of berlaku

DERAI-DERAI TJEMARA (p. 152): In JT and TMT
title: only in TMT
TMT: all lines have initial capitals
TMT: the only end-of-line punctuation is a period after line 12
line 6, TMT: Sudah *lama* bukan kanak lagi
line 10, TMT: *T*ambah *djauh* dari tjinta sekolah rendah

Appendix B

NOTES ON THE ENGLISH VERSIONS

The temptation to discuss all (or at least many) problems of translation is hard to avoid. Since I would in all likelihood find myself writing volumes of extremely detailed commentary if I once yielded to that temptation, I have rigorously kept these notes to the barest minimum. In particular, I have suppressed all discussion of changes made in my previously published versions of Anwar.

INVITATION (p. 13): Although the first line in the manuscript is, as here translated, the single word "Ida," in the poem as first printed this first line was missing.

There is considerable difference of opinion as to whether "Ida" is an abstract construct ("idea, ideal") or the woman journalist and friend of Anwar's, Ida Nasution. I myself favor the latter view though, like everyone else who seems to have speculated on this subject, I lack conclusive evidence.

ME (p. 21): The original title of this poem is as here translated. To avoid difficulties with the Japanese censors, when Anwar read the poem at a July, 1943 Cultural Center meeting, the title was changed to "Spirit," *Semangat*. As H. B. Jassin explains (*Chairil Anwar, Pelopor Angkatan 45*, p. 144): " 'Me' has an individualistic interpretation, while 'Spirit' can be responsibly (and safely) held to concern the collective struggle."

MY HOUSE (p. 39): This is an adaptation of the Dutch poet Slauerhoff's "Woninglooze" ("Homeless"). The Dutch text is as follows:

> Alleen in mijn gedichten kan ik wonen,
> Nooit vond ik ergens anders onderdak;
> Voor d'eigen haard gevoelde ik nooit een zwak,
> Een tent weerd door een stormwind meegenomen.

Alleen in mijn gedichten kan ik wonen,
Zoolang ik weet dat ik in wildernis,
In steppen, stad en woud dat onderkomen
Kan vinden, deert mij geen bekommernis.

Het zal lang duren, maar de tijd zal komen
Dat voor den nacht mij de oude kracht ontbreekt
En tevergeefs om zachte woorden smeekt,
Waarmee 'k weleer kon bouwen, en de aarde
Mij bergen moet en ik mij neerbuig naar de
Plek waar mijn graf in 't donker openbreekt.

EMPTY (p. 41): The poem appears in two sharply different versions. Although in an earlier translation I favored what seems to be the later of the two printed versions (that in *Deru Tjampur Debu*), I have, in retranslating the poem, relied a bit more than I did previously on what seems to be the earlier of the two printed versions (that in *Kerikil Tadjam dan Jang Terampas dan Jang Putus*). Jassin's notes on these textual variations are unfortunately not entirely helpful, though he seems pretty clearly to be in possession of the manuscript (manuscripts?) of this poem.

TO A BEGGAR (p. 53): This is an adaptation of the Dutch poet Willem Elsschot's "Tot den Arme" ("To a Pauper"). The Dutch text is as follows:

Gij met uw' weiflend' handen
en met uw vreemden hoed,
uw aanblik stremt mijn bloed
en doet mij klappertanden.

De letterteekens spelen
om uwen armen mond,
die kommervolle wond
waarlangs uw vingers streelen.

Verhalen moet gij niet
Van uw eentonig leven,
het staat op u geschreven
Wat er met u geschiedt.

Het klinkt uit uwen tred,
het snikt in uwe kluchten,
het sijpelt uit de luchten
waar gij u nederzet.

200

Het komt mijn droomen storen
en smakt mij op den grond,
ik proef het in mijn mond,
het grinnikt in mijn ooren.

Ik zal ter kerke gaan
en biechten mijne zonden,
en leven met de honden,
maar staar mij niet zoo aan.

PRAYER (p. 71): The poem "Jesus Christ" (*"Isa"*) immediately preceding, was written on 12 November; it seems to me to represent a more than usually conscious attempt. "Prayer" (*"Doa"*) written on 13 November and dedicated "to the faithful" (of Islam), is perhaps an equally conscious redressing of the balance—one vote for Christianity, one vote for Islam as well. Note, too, the similarities of form—plain, I think, even in the translations.

FOR THE POET BOHANG (p. 81): Laurens Koster Bohang, a little-known poet, died in Djakarta on 14 February 1945. Like Chairil Anwar, he suffered from syphilis.

It is not clear whether, in the original manuscript, the first stanza is set off in italics; this seems to have been effected only at the time of book publication. When initially published in a journal, further, the first stanza read, in its entirety: "Your voice has the sorrow of the still ocean . . . . . ."

WHISTLING SONG (p. 83): This was at first two entirely separate poems. Part I, dating from November, 1945, was first printed (the next month) under the title "The Moths are Dead" (*"Laron Pada Mati"*) and with the subtitle "Whistling Song: For Ida at Twenty" (*"Lagu Siul: Kepada Ida jang ke-20"*). Part II, dating from February, 1943, was first printed as "No Match" (*"Tak Sepadan"*).

TOGETHER (p. 87): This is an adaptation of the Dutch poet Marsman's "De Gescheidenen" ("The Separated"). The Dutch text is as follows:

De kamer leeg
een vale grauwe nacht
een schemering die aan den dood onsteeg

Wij liggen eenzaam op de zwarte baar
en zullen weldra op de klippen stranden

drijven wij naar den dood
of in de ronde?

de rozen worden zwarter in uw haar

waar zijn uw handen?

A TALE FOR DIEN TAMAELA (p. 99): Having heard many people struggle with the pronunciation, let me simply note that Pattiradjawane is a
six-syllable name, pronounced something like:

pah-tee-rah-djah-WAH-nay.

KRAWANG-BEKASI (p. 127): Krawang-Bekasi is located near Djakarta.
Also known as "Remember, Remember Us!" ("Kenang, Kenanglah
Kami"), this poem is usually read on the tenth of November, National
Heroes' Day (*Hari Pahlawan Nasional*), to commemorate those who were
killed during the independence struggle.

The poem is an adaptation of Archibald MacLeish's "The Young Dead
Soldiers" (*Collected Poems,* 1962, p. 149), which in its most recent form
reads as follows:

The young dead soldiers do not speak.
Nevertheless, they are heard in the still houses: who has not heard
them?
They have a silence that speaks for them at night and when the clock
counts.

They say: We were young. We have died. Remember us.

They say: We have done what we could but until it is finished it is not done.

They say: We have given our lives but until it is finished no one can know what our lives gave.

They say: Our deaths are not ours; they are yours; they will mean what you make them.

They say: Whether our lives and our deaths were for peace and a new hope or for nothing we cannot say; it is you who must say this.

They say: We leave you our deaths. Give them their meaning.

We were young, they say. We have died. Remember us.

SOME ARE PLUNDERED, SOME ESCAPE (p. 151): Anwar used three different titles for this poem: "Some Are Plundered, Some Escape" ("Jang Terampas dan Jang Luput"); "The Plundered and Broken" ("Jang Terampas dan Jang Putus"); and "For Mirat" ("Buat Mirat"). For a discussion of the economic motives which may have prompted these varying titles, see Raffel, *The Development of Modern Indonesian Poetry*, p. 94.

Karet is the cemetery where, on 29 April 1949, Chairil Anwar was buried.

LET'S LEAVE HERE (p. 159): Jassin has in his possession nine of Chairil Anwar's holograph notebooks, from which he prints, in *Chairil Anwar, Pelopor Angkatan 45*, a very few examples of unrevised fragments. There are presumably others: Jassin notes that "there are a number of draft poems, unfinished, missing lines, but some rather long ones, too. . . . Some poems are barely begun [some are partly crossed-out, and so on]. One beginning, 'perhaps a letter'?, seems to be addressed to his ex-wife:

> H,
> I'm all alone in my room. I feel alone
> With my books, again, as before I married you."

Bibliography

PRIMARY SOURCES

Anwar, Chairil. *Deru Tjampur Debu* (*Noise Mixed With Dust*). Djakarta: Pembangunan, 3rd ed.,1953.

————. *Kerikil Tadjam dan Jang Terampas dan Jang Putus* (*Sharp Gravel and Plundered and Broken*). Djakarta: Pustaka Rakjat, 3rd ed., 1959.

————, Rivai Apin, and Asrul Sani. *Tiga Menguak Takdir* (*Three Against Fate,* or: *Three Against Takdir Alisjahbana*). Djakarta: Balai Pustaka, 2nd ed., 1958.

Jassin, H. B. *Chairil Anwar, Pelopor Angkatan 45* (*Chairil Anwar, Pioneer of the Generation of '45*). Djakarta: Gunung Agung, 2nd ed., 1959.

Jassin collects most poems not printed in the three volumes listed above; establishes a reliable working canon of Anwar's surviving work, including a chronological listing; prints Anwar's prose; discusses and prints Anwar's translations of both poetry and prose; discusses the twin issues of Anwar's "plagiarism" and the influence upon him of foreign poets, with poems in several languages.

CRITICISM AND TRANSLATIONS

Damais, Louis-Charles. *Cent Deux Poèmes Indonésiens.* Paris: Adrien-Maisonneuve, 1965.

Contains translations of 14 Anwar poems; a bit flowery but accurate, interesting.

Jassin, H. B. *Kesusasteraan Indonesia Modern Dalam Kritik dan Esei* (*Modern Indonesian Literature: Criticism and Essays*), Volume I. Djakarta: Gunung Agung, 3rd ed., 1962.

Especially important for biographical information.

Johns, A. H. "Chairil Anwar: An Interpretation," *Bijdragen Tot de Taal-, Land- en Volkenkunde,* CXX, 4 (1964).

Excellent literary criticism.

Raffel, Burton. *An Anthology of Modern Indonesian Poetry.* Berkeley and Los Angeles: University of California Press, 1964; Paperbound ed., Albany: State University of New York Press, 1968.

Contains 16 poems of Chairil Anwar, in translations by Burton Raffel, Nurdin Salam, and Derwent May; an enlarged, corrected edition is in progress.

————. *The Development of Modern Indonesian Poetry.* Albany: State University of New York Press, 1967.

Contains a chapter on Chairil Anwar; the first critical history of modern Indonesian poetry.

————, and Nurdin Salam. *Chairil Anwar: Selected Poems.* New York: New Directions, 1963.

Contains an introductory essay by James S Holmes; now out of print; superseded by the present volume.

Teeuw, A. *Modern Indonesian Literature.* The Hague: Martinus Nijhoff, 1967.

Factually accurate, critically weak; deals with poetry and prose, and contains a chapter on Chairil Anwar; contains the most extensive bibliographies now in print.

————. *Pokok dan Tokoh Dalam Kesusastraan Indonesia Baru* (*Themes and Personalities in Modern Indonesian Literature*). Djakarta: Pembangunan, 5th ed., 1959.

Episodic but stimulating criticism; contains a subchapter on Chairil Anwar.